Food for a Better Future

A new direction for the global business of food

SHARON NATOLI

www.sharonnatoli.com

Edition1: First published in Australia by Food & Nutrition Australia, 2018
Author: Sharon Natoli

ISBN-13: 978-0-9758389-1-4

Food For a Better Future: *A new direction for the global business of food*

Cover design and internal design by Stephen Bettess,
Cement Design www.cementdesign.com.au

ACKNOWLEDGEMENTS

This book is inspired by the many people who work in the business of food and who I have had the privilege to work with over the years. The constraints within which you work, your challenges, creativity and expertise have all influenced my perspective and enabled the content that lies within these pages.

I would like to acknowledge all the team at Food & Nutrition Australia, since 1997, in particular Bronwyn Eisenhauer, Janice Kwok and Jade Petitat, for their support and contribution to the many projects that have been undertaken for our clients, and which have contributed to the experiences that have gone into writing this book.

Thank you also to the following:

Lynne Cazaly for your friendship, and for encouraging and inspiring me to commence this journey, Matt Church for creating the structure that has enabled me to crystallise my thinking and believe in my ideas, Peter Cook for your support and commitment to seeing this project through to the finish, Jem Bates for your editing skills and Stephen Bettess for your patience in design and typesetting. Thanks also to Lu Sexton for your early input into the structure of this book and to Dermot Crowley for not giving up on me as this book evolved through its own twists and turns!

To my parents – Lyall and Judy Pelham – you are the wind beneath my wings.

ABOUT THE AUTHOR

Sharon Natoli is an expert in connecting emerging consumer values with corporate and brand values in a way that facilitates long term and sustainable business growth. She is a visionary thinker who strongly believes in the power and influence held within food businesses to create a better future through the way food is produced, marketed and sold.

Sharon is Founding Director of Food & Nutrition Australia (est. 1997) and a sought after advisor to food makers, manufacturers, producers, research and development corporations and franchises. She has qualifications in nutrition and business marketing and for the past 25 years has worked with global and local food brands and producers, including a period working in-house with one of Australia's iconic food brands. She partners with her clients to assist them prepare for the future by sharing her insights and wisdom around the drivers shaping the future of food, working together with her clients to develop food centred values, and leveraging these values to create a meaningful and genuine voice that facilitates trust and connection with consumers in the market.

Sharon maintains regular contact with individuals seeking to change their eating habits, providing her with a grass roots understanding of the drivers behind consumer purchasing decisions and how to communicate in a way that motivates for change.

Sharon believes the current environment in which food businesses operate provides significant opportunity for those looking to enhance performance, to make a difference to the health of the population and the planet, to engage teams and stakeholders, and to remain relevant in the decades ahead.

I believe...

In a world threatened with climate change, rising obesity and social disconnection, the way we grow, produce and consume food provides a powerful solution to many of the challenges we face.

As future generations will increasingly rely on a food system that respects the planet, while nourishing the people it serves, those in the business of food have a great responsibility to get it right.

And I believe we can.

By challenging our thinking and expanding the breadth of what we believe is possible, we can inspire change in a direction that's not only good for business prosperity, but is also good for the future of the planet and for the health of future generations.

Sharon Natoli

FOR ISAAC

May your future be filled with joy and your love for quality food stay with you always. xxx

"We live in a world of content overload. A world where every day 500 million tweets, 4.3 billion Facebook messages and 500 million hours of You Tube footage are sent, posted and uploaded. In this world, only brands that form meaningful connections with people will prosper. It's no longer enough to produce products that work. Brands need to know why people care, and what makes their brands meaningful."

Yannick Bolloré

CONTENTS

"The real question facing us is not 'What do we want to become?', but 'What do we want to want?'"

Yuval Noah Harari

'For the world has changed, and we must change with it.'

Barack Obama

INTRODUCTION

The business and provenance of food is undergoing constant change. Increasing consumer expectations linked to the way food is grown, produced and consumed continue to put increasing pressure on companies to innovate, engage and demonstrate greater responsibility and integrity. A noisy and increasingly fragmented market with greater competition is making it difficult to be heard and more challenging for brands to stand out. A shift in consumer values from the traditional drivers of taste, price and convenience toward sustainability, social impact, health and wellness are creating significant challenges for those in the business of food:

- Many of the products that once were the backbone of consumer's kitchen pantries, are experiencing a deceleration in profit and growth as they struggle to remain relevant.
- Businesses at the maturity stage of their growth phase are seeing their previously innovative products and concepts lose ground as smaller, more agile players enter the market with product and concept offerings more closely connected, and reflective of consumers evolving values.
- A price sensitive food retailing culture creates barriers to innovation making it difficult to create high quality products that maintain consumer engagement and uphold the integrity of brand promises and positioning.
- A clutter of 'me too' products puts the squeeze on retailing shelf space creating high levels of stress for innovators, marketers and sales teams.
- A business as usual approach to marketing and innovation is not creating the differentiation needed to stand out and earn a high-profile position in the retailing landscape.
- Consumers are looking to build real relationships with brands and are turning away from the influence of traditional advertising and marketing.

These challenges sit against a backdrop of rising consumer expectations about how businesses conduct themselves. Society is increasingly demanding a shift from a profit at all costs approach to one that demonstrates a greater role in influencing positive change within the markets in which businesses operate. The move from profit to purpose is escalating as both consumer tolerance for high returns without contribution continues to decline, and leading investors and academics call for a change in thinking.

This evolution in expectations is further indicated by research that found more than 8 in 10 millenials are looking to companies to make public commitments to good corporate citizenship.[1] Those that have taken steps in this area are gaining traction and creating greater connection with consumers. In fact, companies that demonstrate a purpose above and beyond just satisfying consumers functional needs, and are more meaningful, have outperformed the stock market by 206% over a 10 year period.[2] Given millenials have the most spending power of any generation, the investment in being meaningful is set to generate a 'return on integrity' across many areas of business in the years ahead.

For food businesses, one way to enhance brand meaning is to genuinely stand for something greater than the product you produce, grow or sell. Developing and adopting values connected to the food you make and market is a compelling and authentic way to do this and this book shows you how. By developing your unique food values and creating a food philosophy that is communicated genuinely with the market, implemented and progressed, those in the business of food can:

- Create greater brand meaning
- Enhance consumer trust and loyalty
- Grow an authentic brand voice
- Increase stakeholder engagement
- Demonstrate business consciousness
- Enhance organizational culture
- Make better and faster decisions
- Differentiate in the market

For those in the business of food, genuinely connecting with consumers evolving values provides significant opportunity to embrace the changing mood of society. This not only contributes to a better future for business, but a better future for people, the planet and future generations.

The first part of this book outlines the mega-changes that are converging to create a vision of how the landscape for food businesses will change over the coming decade. This vision sets out the rationale for embarking on the journey to build a higher social purpose into current operations that is centred on your food. Part 2 provides a framework for the development of food centred values that will take your business from a 'me too' position in the market to one that is meaningful and Part 3 outlines the importance of communicating your values by identifying and elevating the voices of your passionate experts. Part 4 then summarises the 'return on integrity' that can be expected because of this process, including examples of food businesses that have experienced success, satisfaction and enhanced performance associated with operating according to a set of values centred on their food. Figure 1 summarises this structure.

Finally, I believe of all the players in the food space who aim to influence population eating habits and food production practises, those in the business of food have the greatest power to inspire positive change. The current environment provides a unique opportunity to do this in a way that leads toward a better future for business, for consumers' health and for the health of the planet.

Figure 1: A vision for the future of food. Inspired by food centred values, influenced by passionate voices and lead by those who believe in a better future.

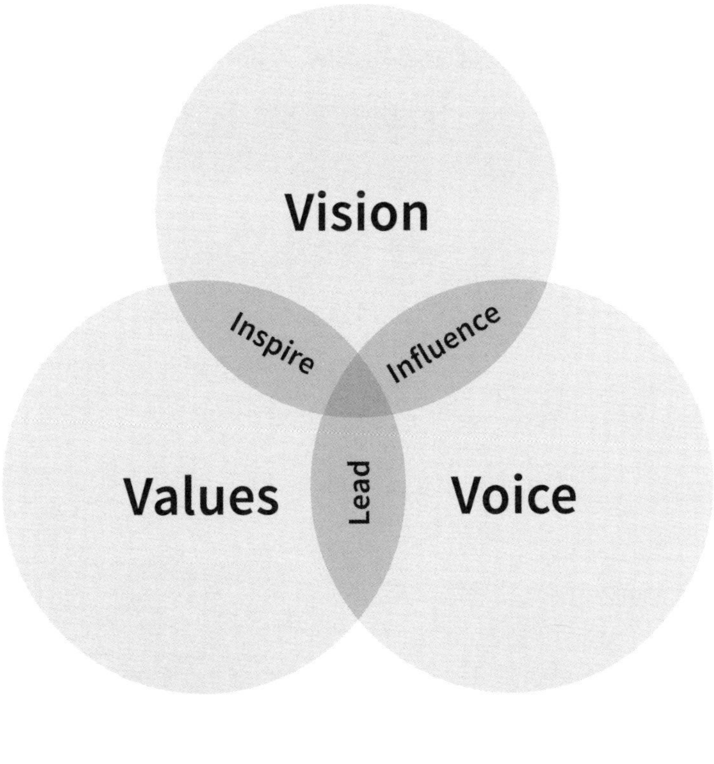

'It's not what the vision is, it's what the vision does.'

Peter Senge

PART 1:
A VISION FOR THE FUTURE

'Our job is not to decide the future; our job is to leave the future as many options as possible'.

Alex Steffen

'We're headed for a climate that has never before existed in the whole history of agriculture. The crops are on the front line. They're the first things that are really going to experience climate change and they're not adapted to conditions they've never seen before. Our domesticated crops are totally dependent on us. Their survival depends on us. That's our future. Like it or not. We're together.'

Cary Fowler

CHAPTER 1

GLOBAL PATTERNS OF CHANGE

From retail, to travel, accommodation to pet care, our commercial world is being transformed at an accelerating rate.[3] And the business of food has by no means been left out. Large food businesses, once the main supplier for the consumer's kitchen pantry, are today experiencing slower growth rates and declining profits. Changing consumer expectations about what their food will deliver are putting increasing pressure on companies to innovate, engage with customers and act responsibly, while technology threatens traditional retail outlets as it offers greater choice around the way we buy, grow and access food. Small food providers, by contrast, being more agile and responsive to changing consumer sentiment around food, are growing on average at five times the rate of their larger counterparts.[4]

Climate change, meanwhile, is threatening our food production, with some of the world's most important staple crops facing declining supply. Global production of major crops such as maize and wheat have already been below expectations, and maize production in Africa is predicted to decline by as much as 22 per cent by 2050.[5] In Australia, a University of Melbourne study found that a warmer climate will have wide-reaching consequences and will severely threaten crops such as chickpeas, walnuts and peaches and lead to a reduction in dairy milk quality and cheese production.[6]

Limited foresight has led to critical loss of crop biodiversity, threatening our ability to feed the world's population, which is expected to climb to 9.8 billion over the next 30 years.[7] At the same time, more and more people globally suffer from overweight and obesity, and food companies are blamed for their role by promoting overconsumption of unhealthy foods and drinks.

Global forces influencing the nature of the food supply are converging with changing expectations about the way businesses should operate. Concern about the role of business in communities and society is putting unconscious capitalism under scrutiny and businesses looking to maximise profits at all costs are struggling to engage. The banking industry is a good example. Tolerance is running out for a culture that focuses on the achievement of record profits while many customers face financial pressure and strain. As a result, the head of business banking for one of Australia's major four banks has recently left his position in the company to start a new bank with a 'back to the future' approach that focuses on a return to relationship banking and a priority to serve small to medium-sized businesses. Responding to the sales-driven culture of the big banks, the new start-up states it doesn't believe in the profit push culture and will not have sales targets. It is set to disrupt an industry that has been seen to be far too heavily focused on profit at all costs.

Similarly, around food, tolerance has run thin for misleading or deceptive marketing practises and for the promotion of unhealthy foods in environments such as schools, health facilities and sporting venues. Concern about unethical treatment of animals and the impact of food production on the environment, and a desire to take greater control of personal health through lifestyle changes rather than medical management, are all putting pressure on food businesses to evolve their practises. Like a sports team preparing for the grand final, many have put in place steps to prepare for the future, but the uncertainty of the opposition and the conditions of match day remain out of their control.

These changes are driven by many factors, not least mainstream acceptance of the impact of human activity on the health of the planet and the increasing burden of chronic disease.

The food system is a key contributor to, and victim of, climate change, and our diet is a key influencer of the prevalence of chronic disease. Given that these macro changes in population and planetary health are overlaying changing consumer and business consciousness, the future survival and prosperity for those in the business of food will rely on operating in a way that demonstrates a greater level of consciousness in the market.

It will no longer be acceptable to purposefully set out to encourage people to over purchase or overeat, or to mislead consumers with clever marketing tactics or bypass codes of practice that protect children from the influence of brand advertising, or to produce food in a way that harms the planet. Consumers won't accept such practices, and for many, a business-as-usual approach will not produce the success that food businesses are seeking in the long term. Future survival, both commercial and societal, requires new thinking and a new leadership approach. For food businesses, this will increasingly mean taking greater responsibility for playing an active role in implementing initiatives that lead people and the planet toward a better future — one that is based on moving from the old world approach to the new world approach as outlined in Table 1.

Table 1: Old vs new world thinking

	Old World	New World
Business	Profit	Purpose
Food	Ignorant	Intentional
Environment	Acceptance	Action
Culture	Depletion	Retention
Social	Disruption	Connection
Health	Physical	Spiritual

The remainder of this chapter outlines the evolution in thinking that is occurring, how values are changing across each of these areas, and the relevance of this to the business of food.

Business — from profit to purpose

'Have you heard about the great crusade?
We ran into million's, but nobody got paid.'
Holy Grail, Hunters and Collectors

The value that has been put on wealth and success, as defined by the accumulation of money and possessions, is increasingly recognised as an obstacle in the path to a better future. That such accumulation has not led us to a happier place is witnessed across all sectors of society. In his book *Global Mega-trends: Seven Patterns of Change Shaping Our Future,* Stefan Hajkowicz proposes that one of the key mega-trends for the future will be the choice of *experiences* over accumulation of possessions.[8] Rising interest in the minimalism philosophy, tiny houses, recycling and repurposing are signs of a shift away from the prestige once associated with material possessions. Today more of us understand that spending more time with people, participating in experiences, enjoying nature and consciously caring for our planet are more rewarding and meaningful ways of living our lives. This evolving change in our consciousness is having an influence across the business community too.

BlackRock, the world's largest investment firm, is responsible for US$1 trillion of investment funds. In January 2018, BlackRock's founder and chief executive called on business leaders and their companies to do more than simply strive for profits. The mood of society is changing around social responsibility, he argued, and now demands that businesses, both public and private, serve a social purpose.[9]

Here was the world's largest investment company challenging the very companies it invests in to engage with the community and embrace a greater sense of purpose. It was a clear signal that a shift toward greater corporate consciousness is pervasive and rising.

Several converging factors are driving this change. Firstly, certain demographic sectors are set on doing meaningful work and therefore seek employment with businesses that demonstrate a purpose they can relate to. In his book *Drive: The Surprising Truth about What Motivates Us*, Daniel Pink talks of how two key generations, baby boomers and millennials, are shifting the centre of gravity in organisations by not rating money as the most important form of compensation.[10] Today they are more likely to choose to work for companies that can offer them a place in 'a great team' or the opportunity 'to give back to society' through their work. Businesses that operate 'not only for profit' are becoming increasingly valued as places to work.

Secondly, changes in human intelligence may be increasing demand for greater business consciousness. The Flynn effect, a term used to refer to the finding that IQ is rising by 3–4 points per decade[11], may be contributing to people's dissatisfaction with mundane, repetitive work and their desire for work that is fulfilling and meaningful. It is surely driving people to seek out businesses with meaningful missions.

This is not unique to one industry but rather is a cross-industry evolution. Fast fashion stores are recognising their contribution to land fill and installing recycling bins in stores to facilitate re-purposing of fabric. The banking industry recently started an advertising campaign that emphasises 'putting people before profits' and contributing to local communities. A major gas provider in Australia is promoting its switch to renewable energy. A men's clothing brand is incorporating diversity in its models and advertising and including messages on its shopping bags about reusing the bag before recycling it. Ikea has committed to producing as much renewable energy as the business consumes by 2020; it is also working with cotton farmers to adopt more sustainable practices while still maintaining a profit. KeepCup, a reusable coffee cup launched in 2009, experienced a 400% lift in sales after the TV program 'War on Waste' was aired and highlighted that standard takeaway paper coffee cups are not recyclable.

Businesses advancing in this direction are starting to reap the rewards, not only in relation to social return on investment, but also in financial returns. The 2017 *Responsible Investment Benchmark Report* found an increase in the number of asset managers using responsible investing as a core theme from 69 in 2016 to 74 in 2017, with the number of investment products offered by these managers increasing from 128 to 224 over the same period. The Responsible Investment Association reported that more Australians want their investments to align with their values, in particular those based on making a positive social or environmental impact. The report also found that funds based on responsible investment strategies generally performed better than equivalent Australian or international share funds.[12]

In the food space, Whole Foods Market in the US has operated with purposeful food-related values since its inception and has reaped the rewards both socially and financially. The company commenced operations in 1980 and 37 years later was sold to Amazon for US$14 billion. Among its food related values are quality standards that include a commitment to feature foods that are free of artificial preservatives, colours, flavours, sweeteners, and hydrogenated fats. The company is also committed to upholding animal welfare standards, reducing the use of pesticides in fresh foods and flowers, sourcing first from farmers who grow food using sustainable practises and providing fresh, wholesome and safe food that supports health and wellbeing.

Wholefoods takes an active role in influencing the broader environment in which it operates by supporting food related projects and initiatives across its supply chain and through its Whole Kids Foundation, Whole Planet Foundation; and the Whole Cities Foundation. Examples include increasing access to nutritious foods in the communities in which the company operates and the provision of microloans to entrepreneurs for projects that help to lift people out of poverty in the 69 countries where the company sources its products.

A study that included a comparison of financial performance of brands under the Unilever umbrella also confirms the value of conscious marketing and business practice within the fast moving consumer goods market.[13] Brands that had integrated sustainability into their purpose and products, were responsible for 70 per cent of the company's growth in 2017.[14]

While it would be easy to imagine that purchasing products based on their sustainability or social purpose credentials is a phenomenon peculiar to developed countries, this is not the case. An earlier study by Unilever also found that 88 per cent of respondents in India and 85 per cent of those questioned in Brazil said they felt better when buying products that are produced sustainably, while in the US the figure was 78 per cent and in the UK 53 per cent.[15]

Speaking about the research, Unilever's Chief Marketing and Communications Officer said: *'This research confirms that sustainability isn't a nice-to-have for businesses. In fact, it has become an imperative. To succeed globally, and especially in emerging economies across Asia, Africa and Latin America, brands should go beyond traditional focus areas like product performance and affordability. Instead, they must act quickly to prove their social and environmental credentials and show consumers they can be trusted with the future of the planet and communities, as well as their own bottom lines.'*

In July 2018, four of the world's largest food companies initiated further action in this area. Nestle USA, Unilever USA, Mars Inc and Danone North America together formed the Sustainable Food Policy Alliance. The group aims to undertake advocacy and action to influence public policies around what people eat and how it impacts their health, communities and the planet.

Evidence is mounting for the benefits of adopting and demonstrating a higher level of consciousness as a long term strategy for business prosperity.

Food — from ignorance to intentional

'Obesity and related illnesses are a greater threat to our quality of life than war, infectious disease and terrorism.'

Yuval Noah Harari

Obesity levels worldwide have tripled since 1975, and most of the world's population now live in countries where overweight and obesity kill more people than underweight.[16]

The alarming rise of obesity and its consequent effects, both physical, social and mental, have at least meant that people are becoming more aware and more informed about the role of food in health. We are moving from a place of willing acceptance and a degree of ignorance about the safety, health and ethics of the food supply to a recognition that everything is up for critical scrutiny. The digital revolution has empowered people by giving instant access to a vast resource of knowledge and information and, with this, a greater level of confidence to question our purchases, not least what lies behind the food we are eating. We want to know why we or our children are gaining weight or lacking energy and are looking for ways to address these conditions through lifestyle changes.

Saturation media coverage by opinion leaders around food and nutrition, along with questionable marketing tactics and a lack of agility on the part of some food businesses, has driven consumer trust in the food supply to a new low. While a few decades ago people were willing to believe the food they were buying, and eating was safe, nutritious and sourced from a food system that could be trusted, this is no longer the case.

Innova Market Insights has found that the number one driver of food purchasing decisions in 2018 is the influence of the mindful consumer, highlighting the drive from ignorance to more intentional purchasing patterns.[17] A more mindful food consumer can be defined as someone who wants to know what's in their food, where it comes from, how it was produced and how healthy it is. They are also sensitive to overconsumption, excess and food waste.

Connecting with a more mindful consumer means re-evaluating some of the traditional approaches to food marketing. It means auditing marketing messages that have been traditional mainstays of the selling process — for example, pulling back from the promotion of excessive intakes. Common marketing descriptors such as '50% more', 'stuffed', 'extra-large' and 'giant size' will gradually lose their appeal as people make more considered choices, recognising and actively avoiding the lure of overconsumption. In fact, research by IPSOS shows reducing portion sizes is second on the list of intentions Australian consumers have around how they will improve their diet (after increasing fruit and vegetable intake).[18]

It's not just portion sizes that are in the firing line. A more mindful consumer considers broader ethical questions when deciding where and what to buy. According to research by the goodDog Agency in 2016, 79 per cent of millennials want to buy ethical brands — that is, brands they trust and feel good about.[19] The research found that consumers show greater loyalty to brands that are genuine and authentic and can demonstrate good intentions — around producing foods that contribute to better health and wellbeing, but also around making a positive impact in relation to social and environmental factors. The impact of food production on personal and planetary health, animal welfare, food safety, ethical production, distribution and country of origin are all influencing consumers' food purchasing decisions.

Figure 2 provides examples of current consumer thinking and behaviour when making food purchasing decisions.

Figure 2: The evolving consumer mindset

A sharper focus on intentional consumption provides the opportunity to shift traditional marketing and product development practices to reflect this greater level and depth of interest in food. Supporting consumers by providing more information in these areas is likely to bring greater rewards for businesses now and in the future.

Environment — from acceptance to action

'We razed four corners of the globe for the Holy Grail'.

Holy Grail, Hunters and Collectors.

The impact of human activity on the environment has been debated endlessly, and indeed is still denied by some. However, the 2016 Paris Climate Agreement (signed by 195 countries as of February 2018) and the development and broad commitment to the UN Sustainable Development Goals are two of the strongest indicators yet that the international community recognises the need to move past political argument to an era of action. Spending on renewable energy and sustainable housing and the introduction of carbon taxes are all signs of a world moving from majority acceptance of anthropogenic climate change to practical action around what can be done to slow the rate of environmental destruction.

In *Sustainable Futures: Linking Population, Resources and the Environment*[20], Ian Dunlop, chairman of Safe Climate Australia, points out that unless global policies are ramped up, the current target of limiting global warming to 2 degrees above pre-industrial levels will be unachievable and the world will be on track for an increase of at least 4 degrees. This would likely melt the Arctic and Antarctic ice sheets, which in turn would result in sea levels rising 70 metres, destroying many cities including all coastal Australian cities. The impact on humanity from the sea level rise alone would be catastrophic.

As both a contributor and a victim of climate change, food production has a major role to play in the future of the planet. It accounts for around 30 per cent of the world's total energy consumption and 22 per cent of total greenhouse gas emissions.[21] It is also responsible for significant land clearing, water usage, water contamination, soil erosion, waste and loss of biodiversity.

Having contributed significantly to climate change, food businesses now can slow its impact.

Writing for just-food, Ben Cooper notes: *'If the Sustainable Development Goals capture mainstream public imagination as they already appear to be doing in boardrooms, their potential to be a true game changer will be unquestionable. They have certainly arrived at a time of unprecedented public concern over sustainability issues suggesting awareness could build rapidly.'*[22]

In the past few years, some of the world's largest food companies have incorporated initiatives in this area in their strategic planning. Change is happening with some examples outlined in table 2.

Table 2: From acceptance to action — global food businesses that have made environmental commitments

Company	Commitment	Examples of goals
Barilla	Good for you. Good for the planet. (launched 2012)	By 2020 Barilla will offer people only products at the bottom of the environmental pyramid. Improve the efficiency of production processes to reduce greenhouse gas emissions and water consumption. Develop projects to promote more efficient and sustainable farming practices for all the main strategic supply chains of the Group.
Mars	'Sustainable in a Generation Plan' (launched September 2017)	Reduce the company's environmental impacts in line with what science says is necessary to keep the planet healthy, focusing on climate action, water stewardship and land management.
Danone	'One Planet. One Health' (launched June 2017)	Eliminate deforestation from the supply chain. Invest in family farmers and projects that restore degraded ecosystems. Invest in programs to reduce and reclaim agricultural waste.
Nestlé	'Nestlé in Society Commitments Plan' (launched 2016)	Provide climate change leadership. Reduce food waste and loss. Improve the environmental performance of the company's packaging.
Unilever	'Sustainable Living Plan' (launched 2010)	By 2030, halve the environmental footprint of the making and use of our products as we grow our business.
Campbell Soup Company	'Environmental Sustainability Policy' (dated 2013)	Reduce the environmental footprint of the company's product portfolio by half, as measured by water consumption and greenhouse gas emissions per tonne of food produced.

In an article for the *Wall Street Journal* in January 2017[23], the CEO of Unilever, Paul Polman, referred to the current food system as 'broken' and needing fixing — a major admission from one of the world's largest food businesses. He argued that *'as producers, manufacturers and retailers of most of the world's food, business has a responsibility to help drive the much-needed food-system transformation'*. The CEO of Danone, Emmanuel Faber, has also urged the food industry to join a 'movement' that aims to *'nurture the adoption of healthier and more sustainable eating and drinking habits'* in a speech to a Consumer Goods Forum in Berlin in 2017.

Adopting environmental commitments is increasingly being accepted as good for business as well as being good for the planet.

Many smaller-scale food businesses have seen this change and launched their concepts on a foundation committed to producing food in an environmentally sustainable way and as a result, are experiencing real growth. Sweet Earth Natural Foods was launched in the US in 2012 on a platform of honouring and sustaining the land and protecting the coast while producing foods that recognise the cultural connection with the land. Within four years the company had experienced phenomenal growth to achieve a US$25 million turnover, before being purchased by Nestlé for an undisclosed sum in September 2017.

Laneway Greens, a small business in Melbourne Australia, launched in 2015 with a food philosophy that includes a belief in seasonal supply rather than consumer demand, and local sourcing to support the local community.

Fish and seafood has been an early adopter category of sustainable production practises that have been well communicated to consumers. Demand for sustainable fish and seafood has long been a driver of purchasing decisions in both the supermarket and the local fish shop. This is demonstrated through research that shows 75 per cent of Australian consumers believe that to save the oceans we need to eat fish from sustainable sources.[24] The same research found that across 21 countries, sustainability was rated more highly than price or brand. This has driven companies to support sustainable fishing practices in their production system, particularly for canned fish such as tuna, salmon and sardines. Safcol, a seafood supplier based in South Australia, has for many years maintained a commitment to 100 per cent pole- and line-caught tuna and FAD-free skipjack tuna, meaning all the tuna product the company sells is produced using responsible fishing methods.

Environmental action is infiltrating investor decision making too. Investors are starting to put greater pressure on food companies to provide evidence of how they are managing risks in their supply chain associated with climate change. A 2017 report by Ceres listed 130 sustainability-focused resolutions filed by food and beverage companies in the six years between 2011 and 2017, up from a handful in 2011 to 23 in 2017.[25]

Sustainable food production increasingly shapes both value-driven consumer purchasing decisions and shareholder investment decisions.

The food service and hospitality sectors are also acting, primarily at the consumption end of the equation, to address food waste reduction. Hyatt Hotels in the US have partnered with global design firm IDEO to assess ways to reduce food waste from the hotels' buffets. Recognising that hospitality businesses such as hotels and restaurants contribute 40 per cent of the 63 million tonnes of food that is wasted each year in the US, the partnership was formed to develop ways of addressing the problem. For business, food waste is not just a waste of environmental resources but also a huge cost. Some interesting and concerning statistics have come out of the project to date.

It has been found, for example, that guests eat just over half of the food set out, and only 10 to 15 per cent of this surplus can be donated or repurposed. Initiatives being trialled to address this issue include smaller sample plates in place of large platters, smaller portion sizes of cakes and desserts, finger pastries instead of whole cakes and single serves of yoghurt rather than large bowls. Implementing just these changes, the project has already generated a cost saving of 10 per cent — without raising any objections from guests.

This is a win–win result, with business taking the lead to reduce environmental impact by reducing food waste while also boosting profits. Environmental sustainability is not just a nice-to-have but is a critical factor in our ability to feed future generations healthy and nutrient rich food. Now is the time to move from acceptance of the role that food production and consumption has to play, to a time of action.

Culture — from depletion to retention

Culture: from the Latin word 'colere' which means 'to care'.

As the world becomes smaller through technological advancements and travel affordability, many aspects of human culture that connect us are becoming less differentiated and more homogeneous. Unique features that defined cultures in the past, including language, ritual, diet, food preparation techniques and connections with the land, are at risk of being eroded. Actions are now being taken to address some of the risks proposed by depletion of cultural assets and to raise our consciousness about steps that can be taken to retain them. The cultural aspects of food, and the ability to maintain and preserve languages, are two important examples.

Retaining language diversity is an important facilitator of the preservation of cultural assets that are passed down orally from generation to generation. It is also critical to our ability to think in different ways. Associate Professor of Cognitive Science at the University of California San Diego, Lera Boroditsky has been studying the interaction of linguistics, psychology, neuroscience and anthropology, and has demonstrated the important role language plays in shaping the way we perceive and interpret the world. The ability to think differently and to see the world from a variety of perspectives is critical to our future prosperity, in particular in areas such as problem solving. A current challenge however is that while there are 7,000 languages spoken around the world, we are losing them at the rate of one language each week.[26] If this continues, it is estimated that half of the world's languages will have disappeared within the next 100 years. This is not only a threat to our linguistic diversity and ability to think differently but is a critical threat to the loss of historical aspects of cultural identity that are reliant on the particular meanings attributed to them through language.

Similarly, as our world gets smaller, many aspects of food culture are at risk of loss, or extinction. This includes not only loss of access to traditional foods and ingredients but also loss of the skills linked with food sourcing, preservation and preparation. The threat of losing cultural aspects of food presents a risk to both collective and individual identity given food can be a powerful symbol of who we are.[27]

Modern lifestyles have seen the rise of a food culture that places a lower degree of value on the important role food plays in the fabric of our daily lives. This presents a critical threat to personal and planetary health. A culture of eating on the run, snacking rather than sitting down to a meal, and the consumption of foods every day that once were considered 'treats' or foods reserved for 'feast days' or special occasions is now commonplace. Shopping, cooking and eating have been put on fast forward as we now order home delivered meals and groceries, microwave single meals to eat on the couch alone, or munch our way through portable foods in the car as we prioritise the need to get somewhere, over the need to be nourished. One of the consequences of this altered food culture is that we are now eating beyond planetary health and personal needs and the lack of attention to what and how we are eating is lending itself to further promotion of overweight and obesity.

Such a food culture also creates demand for quick, cheap and convenient food that in turn drives an over-reliance on a handful of crops and a limited number of animal species. As a result, it has been estimated that 75% of the genetic diversity of domestic agricultural crops has been lost between the nineteenth and twentieth centuries. Seventy five percent of the global food supply now comes from just 12 plant species with rice, maize and wheat alone providing 56% of the energy obtained from food.[28] The world has over 75,000 edible plants but just 200 are used regularly. Similarly, only 15 mammals and bird species account for 90% of animal agriculture.[29]

Preservation of traditional cuisines and their signature ingredients and recipes is one way to work towards maintaining and promoting biodiversity. This is particularly important as climate change starts to influence the types of foods that can be grown effectively due to altered environmental conditions.

There are some positive actions that are being taken to preserve aspects of culture linked to traditional dietary patterns and rituals. In 2013 UNESCO registered the Mediterranean diet as an intangible cultural heritage asset. The traditions associated with the Mediterranean diet and identified as being critical to preserve include the knowledge, skills, rituals and symbols associated with growing crops, fishing and raising animals, along with food preparation, cooking and processing methods. All aspects of food culture are recognised as important, including its social aspects, such as sharing food as a core foundation of cultural identity and connection between communities. All these elements are relevant contributors to the health benefits seen with a Mediterranean eating pattern. Recognition of these broader aspects that define the relationship between the people of the Mediterranean and their food, highlights that eating in a way that enhances health is not just about the type of food consumed, as is often promoted by popular 'diets', but is also about the social and cultural traditions and rituals associated with food and eating.

Cultural preservation is like poring over an old family photo album - we feel a sense of nostalgia and connection. Preserving the richness of diversity, beauty and knowledge of the past and maintaining connections to our roots is a widely felt human need. It also has a positive influence on health, particularly on improving the social aspects of health and wellbeing and on our ability to think and see the world from different perspectives. Traditions and culture reinforce integrity, trust, pride and a sense of belonging.

Culture matters and is increasingly being recognised as an area worth elevating, valuing and preserving and an aspect of our lives where we need to move from the threat of depletion, to one of retention. Food can play a significant role in retaining and embracing different cultures and cultural connections, in turn enhancing the richness of our lives, our health and the health of the planet.

Preserving the culture of food – "Whatever you do, give back more than you take".

Jock Zonfrillo, of the restaurant Orana in Adelaide, is a leading advocate of Aboriginal food culture. Jock established his award-winning restaurant based on a commitment to preserving and elevating respect for local native foods and celebrating the culture and traditional knowledge associated with them. His restaurant serves local Indigenous produce and aims to stimulate and support Indigenous enterprise. The restaurant also supports the associated non-profit Orana Foundation, established to recognise the unique relationship that exists between Indigenous communities, the land and their food culture. Through this foundation Jock is working together with the University of Adelaide and the Royal Botanic Gardens to develop a database of native Australian ingredients, including their nutritional information, seasonality, medicinal and health benefits, and traditional uses such as how the food was cooked or whether it was eaten raw.

The long term aim of the Foundation is to develop a culture that leads to sufficient demand for native Australian ingredients to create an industry big enough to support a living wage for local Australian Aboriginal communities. Preserving and valuing Aboriginal food culture is a way toward economic, environmental, social and spiritual sustainability.

In an interview with Good Food magazine in February 2018, Jock said; *"I was thinking everyone does cartwheels about the pyramids and the Sphinx and these guys [Indigenous Australians] have been around for 40,000 years longer than the Egyptians making bread and nobody gives a f---. How can you ignore the oldest surviving culture on earth?"*

Social — from disruption to connection

'The sharing of food is the basis of social life.'

Laurie Colwin

The infiltration of technology into the way we live has been one of the most significant changes in our lives in recent decades. Smartphones have provided a tool that enables us to remain connected, 24/7. Phones have become so ubiquitous in our lives that there are now more active phone numbers on the planet than there are human beings.[30] Eighty eight percent of Australians own a smartphone and on average, are checking it over thirty five times a day with 35 percent checking it within five minutes of waking.[31] Computers and Wi-Fi connection enable us to work from anywhere — home, cafés, hotels, trains, planes and on the run. While this ready access to technology has many benefits, including facilitating our ability to stay in touch with loved ones, to provide flexibility in our workplace environment and, not least, to find immediate answers to trivia questions at dinner parties, it also has its downside.

A former Facebook executive, speaking at a Stanford Business School event in November 2017, admitted regretting the part he had played in creating short-term reward loops that have exploited a vulnerability in human psychology, which in turn is eroding the core foundations of human interaction.[32] The intrusion of technology and digital connection into areas of our lives where direct, more natural communication once predominated risks contributing to a breakdown of social structures.

The 2017 Mobile Consumer Survey conducted by Deloitte, found 70 percent of people with a phone use it during meal times with family and friends.[31] This distraction is a potential red flag as traditionally, meals, particularly the family dinner, is a time when people connect face to face to share the events of the day, and exchange family support and advice. Humans are communal creatures, and this natural way of interacting serves a generally unrecognised but critical function in supporting our social and psychological wellbeing.

Research confirms this showing a direct correlation between sharing meals and better family relationships. A study of secondary school students in New Zealand found frequent sharing of family meals was associated with higher wellbeing scores, lower rates of depression and fewer risk-taking behaviours.[33] The authors of this study concluded that family meals may provide a unique opportunity for building stronger families. The seeping of technology into mealtimes — checking messages and social media — creates a distraction that reduces personal interaction and can undermine the health of our relationships.

The potential negative consequences are starting to be felt and recognised. Almost 70 percent of 18-24 year olds now admit using their phones excessively and 50% are trying to limit their use.

While what we eat is often a focus for those claiming the secret to a longer life, social connectedness may actually be the most important factor. Psychologist and columnist for the *Wall Street Journal*, Susan Pinker, suggests this to be the case. In her book *The Village Effect. How Face to Face Contact Can Make Us Healthier and Happier*, she notes research indicating that traditional Sardinian communities, who maintain strong family and social connections, have more than ten times as many centenarians as North America. She sees social isolation as the public health risk of our time. Referring to research by Julianne Holt-Lunstad that assessed various aspects of lifestyle and their association with a long life, she found the top two predictors were close relationships and high levels of social integration. The secret to longevity in Sardinia, she argues, lies in the constant interactions of traditional village life and the face to face contact that is a strong part of the culture.

This contrasts with Britain where 10 years ago the first 'safe text' street was created, complete with padded lampposts to protect walking mobile phone users from being hurt when texting. In my own experience of working in Sydney's CBD, negotiating the streets can be akin to playing dodgem cars, having to stay alert to unpredictable pedestrians distracted by their phone screens.

The World Health Organisation recognises the important role that social factors play in influencing long term health and in fact, there is a whole discipline devoted to the social determinants of health. Humans are very sensitive to their social environment and this environment can support or hinder other health related behaviours that are linked to wellbeing.[34] The way we eat and the choices we make are influenced by both social disconnection and by our social connections and networks.

Marks and Spencer in the UK are one company helping facilitate social connection through food. The company has opened 'Frazzled Cafes' in eleven of their stores as a place for those feeling overwhelmed by busy lifestyles to share their stories and be heard while sharing a meal and a cup of coffee.

Similarly, within communities, eating alone is a recognised risk factor that interferes with older people's ability to eat well. In Tasmania, the Eating with Friends project, was established out of a concern by volunteers that many older people living at home alone were eating poorly. The project was established to bring these people together to eat and as a result, is making a difference to their nutritional intake and overall health and wellbeing.

Sharing food around a table (with mobile phones remaining firmly switched off!) is a solution that provides an opportunity for reconnection. MasterFoods have recognised this in their 'Let's Make Dinnertime Matter' campaign, as have President's Choice with their #EatTogether concept. The shift from disruption to connection as a pushback from lives overwhelmed by technology is underway. Sharing the cooking and preparation of food and eating with others around a table plays an important role in facilitating social re-connection.

Health — from physical to spiritual

'Health is a state of complete physical, mental and social wellbeing, and not merely the absence of disease or infirmity.'

World Health Organization

In western cultures, health has traditionally been defined principally in physical terms. If someone has low levels of cholesterol, normal blood pressure and no obvious symptoms of disease, we may refer to them as healthy. Each of these factors, among others, has a role to play in good health; however, we are now feeling that relying on a physical assessment of health alone is limiting and are adopting a broader, more holistic understanding of what it means to be healthy.

Research by Mintel in 2017 found young people are not only focusing on eating well and exercising regularly but are also incorporating mental and spiritual practices in their health regime. Participation in disciplines such as yoga and meditation that have long traditions in eastern cultures, while remaining relatively niche in western cultures, are now being adopted widely for their recognised health benefits. To some extent they are replacing hard-core activities such as marathon running and mountain climbing as people move toward a more balanced and relaxed approach to exercise. This broader definition of what it means to be healthy is also reflected in the way we now define healthy food. A food that is considered 'healthy' is no longer one that is characterised simply by the presence or absence of a nutrient or handful of nutrients. There is increasingly a shift toward a more wholistic definition that incorporates not just the physical or nutritional attributes of a food but where it comes from and how it is made. This is a critical shift for food marketers as while the physical attributes of food will remain an important part of the equation, alone this will increasingly no longer be enough to connect effectively with consumers.

Smaller food makers are starting to make this shift. 13seeds, a hemp farm in Tasmania, for example, include on the packaging of their hemp porridge, an invitation for consumers to visit their farm anytime to see how they do what they do and to hear why.

Traditional foods that have a sense of place and history of consumption are also seen as better for you. Demand for Indigenous Australian bush foods is currently outstripping supply as people's interest in foods that have a traditional and spiritual connection with the land rises. The Gourmet Traveller Restaurant of the Year for 2018 was Orana, a restaurant in Adelaide, South Australia based on a philosophy that honours Australia's varied food history. The menu is based on the Aboriginal philosophy to heal and be healed by the land, and to always give back more than you take. It also celebrates the nutritional properties of indigenous ingredients and respects the relationship between the produce and the land. *See 'Preserving the Culture of Food' on page 21.*

This contrasts with traditional food marketing approaches that focus primarily on the physical aspects of food as a way of categorising whether they are healthy or not. Front-of-pack labelling systems, such as the Health Star Rating in Australia, are an example. This scheme has been embraced by many food makers with a view to help people eat better and to make healthier choices more obvious.

However, the Health Star labelling scheme is yet to prove its value in changing nutrient intakes and improving health and nutrition in the population (a challenging outcome to demonstrate). One of its challenges is that by not considering broader ecological aspects of food it will struggle to keep up with evolving nutrition science, and with consumers evolving definition of what it means for food to be 'healthy'. In the long run, this risks further exacerbating the lack of trust in the food system.

This is starting to be realised by some participants in the scheme. In their two-year evaluation of the system, the Heart Foundation found that while many companies felt the Health Star rating accurately reflected their products, they were concerned about the ability of the scheme to accurately reflect its 'healthiness' and noted that it didn't consider the degree of processing a product has undergone. Some companies expressed concern that these 'inconsistencies' had the potential to reduce consumers' trust in the system.[35]

Similarly, initiatives that set nutrient targets for product 'renovations' and improvements in a company's portfolio have been met with varying levels of sales success and consumer acceptance. In 2016, Arnott's reformulated its leading biscuit brand, Shapes, to improve its nutritional profile. Sales fell, and now they have two versions on the market.

Setting nutrient targets is relevant for some processed and pre-prepared foods as part of an overall mix of initiatives and commitments however it is critical to complement this with an awareness of how consumers and science are evolving. On their own, nutrient targets are no longer enough. Programs that remain focused on evaluating the 'healthiness' of a food based simply on a handful of ingredients and nutrients may struggle for relevance in the future. Being smarter about meeting consumers' changing expectations by taking a broader approach to the definition of what's considered 'healthy' — one that involves a greater depth and breadth of experience and understanding about food, and a more informed approach that focuses on the broader role of food within the ecological environment in which it exists, will be a more effective way to prepare for the future.

ANJA - A Systems Approach to 'Healthy' Food

The food and beverage company ANJA GmbH & Co. KG (Adaptive Nutrition, Joint Achievements) based in Hamburg, Germany, was co-founded by Marc Buckley, an advocate of the United Nations Sustainable Development Goals. The business makes drinks, bars and shakes from organic, fair trade, non-GMO and vegan ingredients. Marc Buckley believes a systems approach to food production is necessary to enable the achievement of the Sustainable Development Goals by 2030 and that this will involve the development of sustainable infrastructures. As all of the Sustainable Development Goals are inter-related, working on one means you will automatically be working on others. In an interview with Food Tank in 2018, he said a complex systems approach is required to work toward sustainability, rather than the simple, linear approach that is the norm and that puts things in silos and boxes.

ANJA has established a green production facility that is CO2 neutral, has a zero energy balance and grows vegetables exclusively with rainwater by combining innovation, technology, resource recycling and renewable energy.

Marc Buckley's approach to product development at ANJA is that: *"Our product is not our products; our product is how we produce."*

Taking the lead

This chapter has highlighted how rising consciousness around many aspects of current lifestyles is creating a new era of problems and possibilities for food businesses.

The breadth of our evolving consciousness provides a great menu of opportunities to demonstrate business purpose, create meaning behind brands and enhance long term performance. People are increasingly looking to food businesses to take the lead and to guide them to make better food choices.

Of all the stakeholders who play in the food and health space, food businesses have one of the greatest levels of influence over what people eat. Given that most people eat three times a day, or 1,095 times a year, a vast potential exists for those in the business of food to make a positive difference to environmental and population health and to social and cultural aspects of food and eating, while also preparing for long term business success.

To deliver to these rising expectations, it's beneficial for food businesses to determine the role their foods play in each of these areas. It makes sense to create a vision around the future of food and to establish values that underpin this vision. By doing so, a platform is created from which to speak out and to develop strong and lasting connections with consumers. This in turn will serve to enhance long term business performance, strengthen the ability to meet key performance indicators and facilitate long term consumer loyalty.

The key question to consider is whether you believe your business has a role to play in creating greater value for society than simply through the provision of the food you sell and in doing so, position yourself for a long term future. If the answer is no, this book is probably not for you. If the answer is yes, read on.

CHAPTER 2

THE CONSUMER IS AWAKENING

Rising global consciousness and the shifts outlined in chapter 1 are influencing many of the choices we make and the ways in which we live our lives. More attention is being given to business responsibility, the importance of mental and spiritual health, and the re-kindling of traditional skills and crafts as we look for ways to connect and to live with a greater sense of purpose. As our consciousness changes, the values we draw on when making food purchasing decisions are also changing.

Moving the Goal Posts

Just like playing soccer with a small child, when it comes to food purchasing decisions, the goal posts are moving. It is now necessary to re-learn and re-focus on where the changes are occurring and to keep practising the skills needed to adapt to these changes in order to remain competitive.

The shift that is occurring in the factors driving consumers food purchasing decisions are outlined in Table 3. The three traditional drivers of taste, price and convenience are no longer the dominant influences they once were. A 2016 Deloitte report found the number of people who say their purchasing decisions are significantly influenced by the new and evolving drivers of health and wellness, safety, social impact, experience and transparency has grown substantially and no longer reflects a niche market. This change is pervasive across region, age and income, meaning significant numbers of consumers targeted by food providers and retailers are changing in a fundamental and impactful way.

Table 3: Changing consumer values driving food purchasing decisions

Traditional	Evolving
Taste	Health and wellness
Price	Safety
Convenience	Social impact
	Experience
	Transparency

Adapted from Deloitte 2016, The Changing Consumer Value Equation.[36]

One outcome of these changing values is that people are starting to develop greater expectations about their food. They want to understand what's in it, where it comes from and how it's made. In the past, it was easier for food producers to sell products simply by getting them onto supermarket shelves or running a mass media advertising campaign. Consumers were content to be led by the choices they were presented with, to select from what was available, and not to question packaging claims, sources or nutritional value. Today it's not that easy.

Every year more than 4,000 new food products are launched in Australia, and up to 20,000 different items are sold through major supermarkets. At the same time, media consumption habits have fragmented. It's common now for people not to watch any mainstream television or listen to any commercial radio. Yet the myriad of other media outlets means we are living in a world of content overload. Every day 500 million tweets, 4.3 billion Facebook messages, and 500 million hours of YouTube footage are sent, posted or uploaded. To cut through this noise, food providers need to know what people care about, and how to tap into consumers changing values in a way that cuts through the clutter. According to Chairman and CEO of Havas Group, Yannick Bolloré only those brands that form meaningful connections with people will prosper in the future.[2]

Consumers have woken up to food marketing tactics that lack integrity, or are perceived to lack integrity, and their changing values are reflecting this awakening. Understanding how consumer values are evolving, and adapting business practises to meet them, will be critical for future prosperity.

TRADITIONAL VALUES

Losing its flavour - taste

'I am not a glutton — I am an explorer of food.'

Erma Bombeck

Food must taste good for repeat purchase to occur — there are no arguments about that. At just about every new product development meeting and sensory research trial I have attended, the key goal has been to get the taste right. However, the development of a crave-able taste at all costs is becoming increasingly unacceptable.

In his book *Salt, Sugar, Fat*, Michael Moss describes how food companies from the 1950s onward invested heavily in creating foods that tasted so good that consumers found them irresistible and so ate more of them. Back then, certain ingredients in foods, in particular fat, salt and sugar, were optimised to provide maximal sensory pleasure. This optimisation targeted the 'bliss point' — the point at which a food or drink achieves maximum palatability. With increasing competition across the food industry, a great degree of inhouse research focused on this area. Taste was a key driver of product sales and foods were formulated for maximum flavour appeal. The result of the technological and marketing methods employed during that era was that supermarket shelves were increasingly dominated by greater numbers of highly processed, unhealthy, nutrient-poor food products.

Moss describes an industry conference in London in 1991, where a presenter observed:

'Food manufacturers need not fear the implication of pleasure in the word bliss. After all, who among us chooses food based on its nutritional status? People pick products off the grocery shelf based on how they expect them to taste and feel in their mouths, not to mention the signals of pleasure their brains will discharge as a reward for choosing the tastiest foods. Nutrition is not foremost in people's mind when they choose their food. It's the taste, the flavour, the sensory satisfaction.'[37]

Clearly, times have changed. The Deloitte report referred to earlier describes health and wellness as the most important evolving driver of consumers' food purchasing decisions. A stark contrast to this food industry executives view point 30 years earlier.

Interestingly, while researching his book, Moss talked with many food business executives who admitted they would not eat the food produced by their own companies, raising questions about exactly what was going into the products at the time.

Today many food companies employ dietitians in the product development phase, recognising that their products must not only taste good but also contribute nutritional value to the diet. A pursuit to produce food products that taste so good they encourage overconsumption will increasingly be viewed as neither responsible nor desirable.

Hitting rock bottom - price

'The price of food today is really very, very high if you include the health costs.'

Alexander Mueller, Think Tank for Sustainability.

Evolving consumer consciousness is loosening the hold of price as a driver of food purchasing decisions as people become more motivated to make choices that put 'values' over 'value'. For example, 70 per cent of millennials state they will pay more for a product that supports a cause they care about.[38] Price will always remain a key factor in food purchasing decisions and healthy food must be affordable as part of a fair food system, however low-cost products that lack transparency and have a significantly negative social or health impact may struggle in the future.

We are already starting to see that a low price strategy can backfire when the cost of food drops so low that it raises ethical questions. When milk is sold for $1 a litre, people begin to ask: Who is really covering the costs? What about the livelihoods of dairy farmers? How is it being produced? What corners are being cut? What about quality and safety standards? Extremely low prices raise doubts, and people begin to question whether cheap food is really worth the price.

When facing increasing competition however, it is natural for businesses to use lower prices to protect declining market share. In his book *Start with Why*, Simon Sinek describes the use of a low price strategy as a tool of manipulation. He offers the case of General Motors and other US car companies who, in response to increasing competition from Japanese car makers in the 1990s, started offering customers cashback incentives. Although these enticements increased share in the short term, they eroded profit margins to the extent that they had to be dropped, after which sales plummeted. This approach simply created a lose-lose scenario.

The same approach and outcome occurs regularly in the highly competitive grocery market. As shelves become increasingly cluttered and the competition increases, use of price discounting to enhance sales is used frequently. Price promotions move products off shelf for the short time they are on special. This helps the retailer clear stock, however can have devastating effects for the long term viability of brands. Once the price promotion ends, sales plummet, the next brand takes over and people become trained to buy only what's on special. Once this happens, food businesses see their products trapped in a cycle of price promotions, and languishing sales while they are not discounted, and some never actually recover. A review of the Food & Grocery Code of Conduct in July 2018 has in fact called out unfair practises by major Australian food retailers linked to treatment of suppliers. With significant market power, pressure to reduce prices and to cycle promotional activities at the same dollar value every year were considered two key issues requiring cultural change.

In a low price culture, taking a stand against low prices at all costs can provide a point of difference. When the two big Australian supermarket chains were locked in a price war over cheap milk in 2016, Harris Farm Markets, a smaller local retail chain, announced it would not sell milk at this price. To show its support for the local dairy industry, it would stock only its own Farmer Friendly Milk at a minimum price of $2.29 per two-litre carton. This enabled the company to return 95 per cent of the income from milk sales to its suppliers. This move received positive public support and created a strong voice for the brand in the market.

People are starting to show a greater willingness to pay more for foods that reflect their emerging values, rather than being driven to purchase on price alone. Eggs that are produced in an open range system and are marketed locally sell out at a price that can be up to five times as high as cage eggs sold through major retailers. Artisan breads may sell for three to four times the price of standard supermarket breads as people appreciate the time and expertise involved.

The evolution that is taking people over the price barrier and into a realm where the value of food is based on more than its monetary cost is an exciting opportunity for businesses. Moving from competing on price to competing on different definitions of value means businesses can be true to their beliefs while potentially increasing profit margins and gaining long-term loyalty.

Competing on price works well for businesses looking to build transactions, but not for those seeking to build value in other ways. The loosening of price as a key driver of food purchasing decisions provides a significant opportunity for food businesses looking to differentiate beyond short-term price discounting and rewards toward building a following of loyal customers.

The cost of convenience

'It would be perverse to embrace inconvenience as a general rule. But when we let convenience decide everything, we surrender too much.'

Tim Wu

Convenience is another important driver of food purchasing decisions around which perceptions are changing. In an article in the New York Times, Tim Wu challenges our assumption that convenience is always good, arguing that while it promises greater efficiencies, it also 'threatens to erase the sort of struggles and challenges that help give meaning to life'[40]. As we contemplate the introduction of kitchen robots that will have the ability to make our dinner for us, we may well find ourselves reflecting on the value of convenience as an alternative to the expression of love and gratitude that often accompanies a home-cooked meal.

Convenience will remain a key driver of consumer purchasing decisions; however, convenience based on excessive processing is less attractive and less acceptable than it once was. As I will discuss in the next chapter, people are starting to judge the health value of a food based not only on its nutritional profile and list of ingredients, but also on the amount of processing it has undergone. Trading off health for convenience is becoming less acceptable; people are demanding both, as is illustrated by the growth in popularity of home-delivered fresh meals and meal kits.

Businesses offering home-delivered meal kits, such as such as Hello Fresh, Marley Spoon and others, generated $94.5 million in sales in Australia in 2016[41], and sales in the US are expected to reach US$10 billion by 2020.[42] Enabling people to prepare home-cooked meals from fresh ingredients without the hassle of shopping or meal planning strikes an appealing balance between health, freshness and convenience. It also addresses feelings of guilt that can arise when people rely on fully prepared meals.

Like price, convenience may have a floor below which perceptions switch from positive to negative. This is not a new idea. In fact, it was discovered more than 60 years ago by the inventors of Betty Crocker cake mixes. Beginning in 1943, the Washburn-Crosby Company, who owned the brand at the time, spent four years in the product development and testing phases. Their aim was to help busy American housewives prepare home-baked cakes quickly. When the products were finally launched, however, they lacked traction. Feedback indicated that buyers felt guilty about resorting to such a short cut. So, the developers went back to the drawing board and redesigned the cake mixes so they required the addition of an egg, some butter and milk. It seemed that giving the customer a greater role in the cooking process addressed this 'guilt' and ensured a much greater take-up of the product.

This story illustrates the role personal engagement and pride can play in the food preparation and cooking process. For many, cooking and preparing meals continues to be closely linked to care and love of others; it's a nurturing act that provides a sense of satisfaction and empowerment. It plays an important role in facilitating social connections.

The pursuit of convenience has led to drive-throughs, fast food, eating on the run and 'snackification', which has seen regular meals replaced by irregular snacks for many. Research shows that snacking now accounts for 50 per cent of eating and drinking occasions.[43] This shift has particularly affected breakfast and lunch, with people fitting in eating around their work schedules rather than fitting their work around scheduled mealtimes. One result of this trend is that we eat together less. Convenience enables families to microwave meals as required and to eat at different times, with less washing up. While this has its advantages, it can compound the social isolation that is emerging with the distraction of technology.

People are starting to recognise the negative impact on social and mental health that is a consequence of overly busy lifestyles. With the recognition that convenience has a cost, a rebalancing is occurring, part of which is an emerging recognition of the importance of making time to cook and share meals with others.

Growing numbers of people today, frazzled by ever greater distractions and longer to-do lists, are looking for ways they might slow down rather than speed up. One of the signs of this shift is in the nature of the claims used on new food and drink products. In the five years to August 2016, new food and beverage product launches with claims incorporating the word 'slow' grew four times as fast as those that referred to 'on the go' consumption.[44] It seems that notions of 'slow food' and the relaxed and social sharing of food are appealing to people who want a break from their hectic lifestyles. While many of the products using a 'slow' claim still provide convenience, the appeal of slow food likely reflects a changing consumer mindset that associates slowing down with greater care, better nourishment and a reassuring sense of nostalgia. These values are reflective of those established by 'Slow Food', an organisation dedicated to counteracting the rising speed of life by rekindling people's interest in the food they eat and preserving local food cultures and traditions. Like the tortoise in Aesop's tale The Tortoise and the Hare, it seems slow and steady may win the race after all.

Younger people are also embracing this trend toward slowing down and are demonstrating a return to home cooking. In fact, research by Mintel found 31 per cent of 25 to 34-year-olds are spending more time on home cooking, compared with 24 per cent of those aged over 35 years. Younger people are also seeing cooking at home as a path to better health.[45] The rise of the 'normovore', a term coined by chef and author Dave Chang to define Generation Z's more conservative approach to life, includes food, and the return to traditional home cooking.

Similarly, research by Nature found one of the barriers to uptake of ordering food through a meal delivery app was a personal preference by Australian families to cook from scratch. This research found 84% of people had ordered from a meal app once a month or less and 43% had never tried to use one.[46] We may even be witnessing a decline in demand for home delivery services with more people reporting their spending was either the same, or less, than it was a year earlier. Like price, it may be that convenience has a floor and that while it will continue to play a key role in the future, it may be balanced by a recognition that cooking and food preparation play a bigger role in a healthy, balanced lifestyle than simply through the provision of nutrients.

Each of the traditional drivers of taste, price and convenience clearly have their 'costs'. They will remain important but will increasingly share the stage with new and emerging consumer values. Businesses will benefit from continuing to account for the traditional drivers of food purchasing decisions however in the future, it will be critical to pay increasing attention to the new and evolving consumer values that are emerging as key drivers of food purchasing decisions.

The following evolving values are those that increasingly need to be addressed by food businesses looking to remain relevant in the decades ahead.

EMERGING VALUES

Reassure me

'Sugar is now more powerful than gunpowder.'

Yuval Noah Harari

Food safety scares, uncertainty about what's in food and conflicting advice about what to eat for good health are all driving a greater desire to be reassured about the safety of what we are eating.

In his book *Big Fat Lies*, David Gillespie[47] warns us that the diet industry is making us sick, fat and poor. Not only that, exercise won't help us lose weight, and low GI (Glycemic Index) diets are dangerous. In *The Case Against Sugar*, Gary Taubes[48] argues that sugar is 'the tobacco of the new millennium', is deeply entrenched in our lives and is making us very sick indeed. Dr David Perlmutter, in *The Grain Brain*[49], claims eating a gluten-free, high-fat, high-cholesterol, high-fibre diet with virtually no carbohydrate can help combat at least 30 different conditions including ADHD, mood disorders, headaches, memory loss, overweight, infertility, high blood pressure and bad breath. It seems wherever we turn there's someone with the cure for all our health problems — it's just that we've been listening to the wrong advice, eating the wrong foods or accepting the wrong scientific evidence.

This bombardment of information about what to eat means we live in fear of making the wrong food choices. Conflicting advice puts us constantly on guard. Fear and uncertainty are compounded by a wondering about the steep rise in food allergies, concerns about plastic pollution infiltrating the food system, and the unintelligible chemical names found in ingredient lists.

Such worries are further amplified by living at a time when most of the world's increasingly urbanised population is growing up disconnected from the sources of their food. In 2008 the world's urban population exceeded the rural population for the first time in history meaning more people had less interaction and awareness of the process of growing food.[50] This contrasts with 1900 when there were 6.7 people living in rural areas for every one person living in a city. Today more people live in urban areas than the total world population in 1960.

The number of farmers in Australia has also been declining for decades. In 2011 there were 19,700 fewer farmers than in 2006, a decline of 11 per cent over a five-year period.[51] Fewer farmers and higher levels of urbanisation make it more challenging for people to stay connected to the sources of their food. The contribution this makes to fear about food is significant. What we can't see, we find harder to understand.

Doubt and mistrust because of these changes in the environment in which we live means people are seeking reassurance when making purchasing decisions. Use-by dates, place or country of origin, ingredient lists, nutrient content, the presence or absence of additives and allergens are all ways people seek reassurance. The rising sense of alienation from the source of our food has no doubt contributed to the success of school-based programs that teach children how to grow, harvest and cook food, and to the growth in popularity of farmers' markets.

In his book *In Defense of Food*,[52] Michael Pollan proposes that food fears can be addressed by 'shaking the hand that feeds you' meaning trust is earned when you can look into the eyes of the person who grew the food you're about to buy. The Stephanie Alexander Kitchen Garden Program, launched in 2007 with the aim of encouraging children to develop positive food habits for life through the creation of kitchen and garden experiences in schools, is helping to connect children with the sources of their food and has been shown to increase the number of children willing to try new foods. Kimbal Musk, younger brother of business entrepreneur Elon Musk, has created Big Green, a non-profit organisation that aims to build 'Learning Gardens' in low-income schools across America. Celebrity chef Jamie Oliver has long been an ambassador for teaching children to understand where their food comes from and in the process has discovered shocking facts about the consequences of not bringing children up with a contextual understanding of how food is grown and prepared.

Such initiatives are making a difference to the enjoyment, confidence and pleasure children can gain through a greater connection with the sources of their food. They also help reduce the fear and uncertainty that can arise as a result of growing up being disconnected from the source of the food supply. Explaining recipes, sourcing local food, participating in food education and being more transparent are all ways food businesses can connect with growing consumer values around food safety and reassurance.

Emerge in the experience

In his book *Global Mega-trends*, CSIRO strategy and foresight scientist Stefan Hajkowicz identifies seven patterns of global change that he believes will shape the future of business.[8] The changes heralded by mega-trends may lie beyond our direct control, but an understanding of these long term trends provides us with an opportunity to become 'future ready'. One of the seven mega-trends is that of 'great expectations'. This refers to the shift from an economy built on the purchase of goods and services to one that is increasingly valuing experiences. We are becoming more interested in the experiences that surround the purchase of a product and are spending a greater proportion of our discretionary expenditure on non-material things.

Interest in experiences associated with food is evidenced in the excitement we see when our expectations are exceeded by a special home cooked meal or by the way food is served at a new eatery. Food has great potential to offer new experiences, whether through exciting new flavours, cuisines from different cultures or through learning new techniques associated with food preparation and preservation. Classes such as learning how to ferment, make cheese, or how to use all cuts of meat in cooking are growing in popularity.

Businesses are starting to recognise the value of meeting this emerging trend by adopting new ways of marketing that involve teaching and education. Brasserie Bread, a small artisan baker on the east coast of Australia, runs classes on how to make sourdough bread, woodfired pizza bases and how to mill your own flour. According to the company, interest in the classes started small but expanded quickly to a point that was beyond their expectations. The company now plays an active role in educating thousands of students, including primary and senior school students through classes and excursions annually.

The ability of food businesses to teach taps into the desire people have to continue learning throughout life. It can also result in brands holding a special place in consumer's minds while building long term loyalty.[53]

The emergence of 3D printing offers another way to connect with consumers increasing desire for experiences. 3D technology enables the deconstruction and reconstitution of food in a way that enables foods and meals to be tailored to individual preferences and specific nutritional composition. Having inserted into the printer a cartridge containing various food 'pastes', the operator can choose the shape, portion size and design of the food to suit their specific needs.

The world's first 3D printed food restaurant, Food Ink, opened in London in April 2016. Food Ink offers diners the opportunity to experience 3D printed food served with 3D printed utensils on 3D printed furniture. The restaurant, which has also been showcased in various cities throughout the world, aims to provide 'a taste of tomorrow' through combining technology with art, music, poetry, tradition and music.

Some food manufacturers, such as Barilla, have also invested in this space. Showcasing progress with their 3D pasta printer at Expo Milano in 2015 and more recently, giving it the name of BluRhapsody, Barilla are aiming to develop their pasta printing technology to create a portfolio of products for high end applications in the restaurant and catering industries.

Meeting consumers' desire for new experiences doesn't have to be glamorous and high tech, though. Supporting the development of urban gardens and vertical farms that will enable community input and access to a variety of produce at specific times of year will be another way of immersing in food related experiences. Bringing people together to share food in new environments or in association with special events, providing new ingredients or facilitating the ability to try new recipes will also appeal. Significant opportunities exist to build trust and loyalty by meeting consumers growing desire to 'emerge in the experience'.

I want to see all of you - transparency

Innova Market Insights' number one trend for 2018 was the rise of the 'mindful consumer', someone who wants to know where their food comes from, what's in it and how healthy it is. This is a reaction to low levels of trust and, just like someone about to jump out of a plane wanting to know what the weather is like, when to open their parachute and where they are going to land, people now want more information about the food they are buying. It is becoming increasingly important to operate with a transparent, open and honest approach. Recognising that people want to feel connected both physically and emotionally to the food they eat, many food businesses have started to respond with commitments around transparency.

Examples include Lilydale, a producer of free range chicken, who included a picture of a farmer on the packaging of their chicken products and linked this to a bar code that could be scanned by customers to discover the actual farm that produced the chicken. Sunny Queen Eggs offers Chooktracker®, a live stream that shows their free range chickens roaming around their pastures. Hershey's in the US has included an

A–Z glossary of ingredients it uses in its products, with an explanation of the function of each. Campbell's have done a similar thing with their 'what's in my food' website.

Availability of hand held food spectrometers now allows for the molecular identification of the composition of a food, including its nutritional profile, time it was picked and how long it has been stored. This technology means that transparency around food will soon be completely in the hands of the consumer. It will no longer be necessary to rely on marketing claims and information provided by manufacturers and producers. This will have implications for food marketing in the future as transparency will no longer be an option – it will be a given. Now is the time to prepare for this transition.

Don't Hurt or Harm Others – Social Impact

As lifestyles change and our standard of living rises, this allows for more people to have their basic needs met. A consequence of this is that the ability to consider others becomes more prevalent. As a result, people are increasingly looking outward, beyond their own needs, and showing concern around issues such as animal welfare, sustainability, local sourcing and fair treatment of workers when making food purchasing decisions.[36] The number of people exhibiting these concerns is identified as small but growing.[36]

Many of these social impact concerns can challenge business as usual practises as they can have significant cost impacts. This means they can be hard to change. However, research conducted by the goodDog Agency found 79 percent of millennials want to buy from brands that demonstrate an ethical approach so the short term investment will likely be worthwhile.[54] Making changes to address this emerging value now is also positive for brand reputation and team engagement.

One example of the significant influence on sales that consumers emerging values around social impact can generate, is that experienced by the Australian egg industry. With consumers perceiving free range egg production to be more socially acceptable than cage egg production, sales of eggs from each of these systems have changed significantly over the past decade. In 2009, free range eggs represented just 5% of the market but by 2016 this had increased significantly to 40% while cage egg sales declined from 70% to 49%. Awareness of emerging values around how food is produced is therefore a critical consideration for the future, as it can have a significant impact on sales preferences within a market.

Factors that reflect aspects of food production linked to social impact will continue to rise as people consider more than the end product they purchase.

A HEALTHIER FUTURE

Decades ago, 'health foods' were mainly the preserve of hippies and alternative types, who bought organic, unprocessed, additive-free foods in brown paper bags from the local health food store. Today healthy food is no longer a niche market, but rather a key influencer of food purchasing decisions for a majority of the population. A report by IRi Consumer Health found that for at least 62 per cent of people, health is now a key consideration when making food purchasing decisions.[55] This is being driven by greater access to information, education and awareness, and growing recognition of the important link between diet and health.

Research indicates that 83 per cent of consumers globally consider diet and nutrition important to their wellbeing,[56] meaning food products that offer a health and wellness benefit continue to capture an ever greater share of the global food market.

'Better for you' claims continue to increase their market penetration.[57] Recent research by Nielsen found more than 40 per cent of global consumers say they are influenced to purchase foods that are 'all natural' or contain more fruits and vegetables, with around a third favouring foods that are lower in salt, sugar and fat or higher in fibre, protein and whole grains.[57] Sales data shows these attitudes translate into sales. Between 2012 and 2014 sales in both healthy and indulgent food categories grew globally; however, "healthy" rose at more than double the rate of indulgent. Consumer interest in health and nutrition is, as identified by Deloitte, the most important and complex of all the evolving consumer values.[36]

Of relevance to businesses is that more people also say they are willing to pay more for healthier foods and are seeking out more options that deliver to these needs.[59] It makes good sense to focus on developing and marketing healthier foods but being informed about what 'healthy' means is critical to gaining traction and resonating with consumers.

What is 'healthy'?

The definition of what is considered 'healthy' food is changing. Given health and nutrition is the most significant evolving consumer value, it is essential to understand the nature of this change. The evolution from 'now' to 'next' is outlined in Table 4.

Table 4: The evolving definition of 'healthy food'

Now	Next
Nutrient focus	Whole food focus
Free from	Naturally functional
Superfood	Simple and soulful
Physical	Social and mental
The food	The food system
Good for me	Good for me, good for the planet

Nutrient focus to whole food focus

An approach that defines the health and nutritional value of foods on a single or even a handful of nutrients is becoming less compelling for consumers. While 'low fat' and 'diet' were once considered intrinsically healthy, this is no longer the case. In fact, claims such as these can even backfire as people consider what's been added or removed as a trade-off. According to Datamonitor, diets focusing on a single nutritional element will be scarce by 2020.[60] This has been dramatically illustrated by the shifting market share of low-fat and full-fat dairy foods — for example, from low- or no-fat milk to whole milk that is considered to be more 'natural' and 'real'. Sales of whole milk increased significantly enough in Australia in 2017 for retailers to start worrying they would run out of butter.

Free from to naturally functional

Claims such as 'gluten free', 'sugar free', 'dairy free' and 'wheat free' will continue to hold appeal however will give way to more information about what's in the food and what it's going to do for me. Interest in highly nutritious, 'naturally functional' foods such as beetroot, blueberries, chia seeds and turmeric will continue to grow. Over-doing 'free from' claims, such as one product that claims to be 'baked, sugar free, gluten free, dairy free, guilt free, naturally sweetened and low carb' will likely start to generate consumer distrust. There is evidence that people are starting to suffer from 'clean-label fatigue'.

Superfood to simple and soulful

The term 'superfood' has been used indiscriminately by marketers in the past few years without any consistent definition of the term, with the result that people have tired of it. The idea that one food can solve multiple health problems, or claims that are seen as over-exaggerating a foods health benefits, now risk alienating consumers who are responding to more real, genuine and authentic communications. Roy Morgan research has found that Australians are generally fed up with food trends, with 81 per cent reporting that they believe a simple approach to a healthy diet is better suited to the Australian lifestyle. Pushing back from superfoods, younger people are now moving back to simpler, more 'soulful' food.

Physical to mental and social

The shift toward a more balanced and holistic definition of health, as outlined in chapter 1, is influencing the changing way we consider how food contributes to good health. We are seeing the adoption of a broader definition that takes into account not only how food contributes to physical health, but also how food affects mood and mental health, as well as contributing to social wellbeing.

Some food businesses have started incorporating this perspective in their communication and advertising. For example, MasterFoods has made the 'Pepper Hacker' advertisement which highlights the importance of families 'disconnecting to connect.' Laneway Greens, a small food outlet in the centre of Melbourne has a philosophy that includes the belief that food is a chance to connect. Governments in some countries, for example Brazil and Germany, have recognised that encouraging healthy eating patterns includes broader considerations that include the social and mental health benefits of food. The box opposite provides examples of dietary guidelines in these areas as published by Brazil's Ministry of Health.

Extracts from Brazilian Dietary Guidelines

- Diet is more than the intake of nutrients.
- Healthy diets derive from socially and environmentally sustainable food systems.
- Always prefer naturally or minimally processed foods and freshly made dishes and meals to ultra-processed foods.
- Always when possible eat daily meals at similar times. Avoid 'snacking' between meals. Eat slowly, with full attention, and enjoy eating without engaging in another activity.
- Always prefer to eat in clean, comfortable, and quiet places, and where there is no stimulus to consume unlimited amounts of food.
- Prefer eating together with family, friends, or colleagues. At home, share in acquisition, preparation, cooking and arrangements before and after eating.

Dietary Guidelines for the Brazilian Population, 2nd edition, 2014

From the food to the food system

Knowledge about the production system is increasingly influencing how healthy a food is perceived to be. For example, we know fish is good for us, but if it comes from a source we do not trust, we are less likely to purchase it or to consider it healthy.

Food businesses are starting to respond by seeking foods and ingredients from environments considered clean, green and trustworthy and highlighting this in marketing. More information is being provided about the way food is produced and the techniques used in processing, particularly those linked to artisan skills, such as smoking, pickling, baking or fermenting. Provenance claims are increasingly influencing perceptions about the quality of foods, and decisions around whether a food is good for us.

Good for me, good for the planet

Between 2014 and 2016, concern that food production should be conducted in a way that is not harmful to the environment jumped from 8th in a list of high priorities to be the third most important priority for Australian consumers.[18] This rising concern is being driven by some of the factors that are playing on consumers' minds, as outlined in chapter 1. It is also being driven by government attention to the link between food production and the environment.

In 2016 the UN launched its Sustainable Development Goals (SDG), a call to action to end poverty, protect the environment and improve living standards around the world. Signatory countries agreed to work toward achieving an ambitious set of goals by the year 2030. Many of these goals relate to food — the resources that go into producing it, the waste generated, and the disease and adverse social conditions linked to too little, too much or nutrient-poor food. Achieving these goals is now on government agendas and is increasingly influencing government policy setting and business practices. Primary industries as well as manufacturers, franchises and retailers have started to adopt sustainability initiatives and targets. These include initiatives around areas such as water usage, greenhouse gas emissions, food waste and landfill that assist in meeting the UN's Sustainable Development Goals. The horticultural industries in Australia have invested in integrating sustainable soil health practices into commercial vegetable farming. Many large food and beverage manufacturers, including PepsiCo, Unilever, Starbucks, Danone and Nestlé, and others have developed public commitments and targets to support the achievement of the SDGs by 2030.[61]

The Sustainable Development Goals have contributed to recognition at government level that food production and consumption relate closely to both personal and planetary health. The Australian government recently established a Fight Food Waste Co-operative Research Centre and a National Food Waste strategy. It is also expected that the next revision of the Australian Dietary Guidelines will include a greater focus on the environmental impact of healthy diets and will address both personal and planetary health when making recommendations to the public about what to eat.

Addressing members of the European Parliament's Committee on Agriculture and Rural Development in May 2017, FAO Director-General José Graziano da Silva stated that *'nourishing people must go hand in hand with nurturing the planet'*. Acknowledging that high-input, resource-intensive farming systems have substantially increased food production, he observed that such development had nonetheless come at a high cost to the environment.

Food businesses are starting to acknowledge that they can play a role in this as an agent of change. However, a great deal remains to be done, particularly at the consumption end of the equation and in playing a role to lead consumers toward positive changes in habits. This is starting to emerge with examples including initiatives such as imperfect fruit and vegetables being made available for sale through food retailers, juice brands being introduced that use fresh produce that would otherwise be wasted, and companies such as Natural Evolution who have produced banana flour from bananas that would otherwise have gone to waste.

Such initiatives are examples of how food businesses are making a difference and understanding that the drivers of food purchasing decisions are shifting to include not only decisions around whether the food is good for 'me', but also whether it is good for the planet.

Business as usual is not working

When I tell friends I work with the food industry, a common reaction is along the lines of, *'Oh, they need you — they're always trying to tell us their food is healthy when it's not'*. Speaking on SBS television about his 800-calorie diet to reverse diabetes, TV presenter Michael Mosely asserted bluntly, *'The food industry tries to sell us junk disguised as healthy food.'* This encapsulates a widely held public sentiment.

We are living at a time when trust in big business is at an all-time low. This is across many industries however consumer mistrust of the food industry is even higher at 3.4 times the cross-industry average.[36] Millennials are particularly suspicious of the food industry, with 43 per cent reporting that they don't trust large food manufacturers, compared with 18 per cent in a cross-industry average.[36] Given that millennials represent the largest spending generation, this is a considerable problem.

Looking back at some of the initiatives implemented by food businesses and industries over the years, it is easy to understand how this has come about. Take the advertising by the sugar industry in the 1960s, which advised people that eating an ice-cream cone before dinner was a good way to curb the appetite, or the claims in the 1970s that sugar was 'a good food'. In 1942 there were 'Vitamin Donuts', and in 1980 McDonald's assured us a meal consisting of a Big Mac, regular fries and a strawberry milkshake was 'as good for you and your family as it is good to eat' and that 'keeping you and your children in good health makes good sense and good business'. In 2005 Kellogg's highlighted the lack of artificial colours and flavours and the high vitamin and mineral content of its Coco Pops cereal using a Play School celebrity, implying it was healthy despite the fact the cereal was more than a third sugar.

Food businesses can attract unwelcome headlines when taken to task over misleading claims. These stories serve to further harm the reputation of the industry and feed into popular fears and uncertainty. More recently, Uncle Tobys Oats was criticised for a large front-of-pack claim that it was 'rich in protein', when the source of most of the claimed protein was the milk served with the cereal rather than the oats themselves. The courts ruled that this was misleading; the company was fined and required to remove the claim from its packaging. The chairman of the Australian Competition and Consumer Commission (ACCC) commented that oats have many health benefits, but protein is not one of them.

Similarly, Heinz were fined by the ACCC for implying its Kids Shredz product was nutritious for kids when the court deemed it wasn't, based on its sugar content of 60 per cent.

These are just a few examples. Attention and scrutiny around the claims made by food businesses are likely only to increase with the growth of social media and other advances in technology, particularly around spectrometry and blockchain, which will mean ever greater (and better informed) vigilance by consumers and regulatory authorities. Exaggerating what's good, or what a product is 'free' from, without context will continue to be called out in the future. This highlights some of the issues facing food marketers if they become stuck on a business-as-usual course.

The evolution of marketing in a general sense is well covered by Carolyn Tate in her book *Conscious Marketing*, in which she highlights some of the problems that marketing is facing. She argues that marketing has been hijacked by 'the fourth P', *promotion* (after *product*, *price* and *place*), and that this is driving a focus on short-term gains in market share and the simple desire to dominate the competition. This has kept the focus on what other companies are doing rather than on innovation and more conscious ways of marketing. Greater consciousness in marketing is how the industry is now evolving and this approach is complementary to how consumers expect food businesses to operate.

With trust in the food system so low, getting marketing messages right is worth the effort and investment. Research by Mintel confirms that gaining the trust of the younger generation will pay off significantly in customer loyalty. When surveying younger millennials, they found that 60 per cent are brand loyal and that they want companies to connect with them in an authentic and genuine way by reflecting their shared values.[45] The benefits of moving from a business-as-usual approach to food marketing towards one that is more meaningful, and values led is significant.

Who is going to lead?

"Insanity is doing the same thing over and over again and expecting different results."

Albert Einstein

The marketing tactics of the past will become increasingly ineffective for food producers looking to thrive in the decades ahead. Now is the time to take a more active role in helping consumers make better choices, to produce food in a way that considers its environmental impact and to take greater responsibility around how it is marketed. While ultimately people will make their own food decisions, implementing initiatives that improve the way food is produced and marketed, and nudging consumers in a direction that facilitates the selection of better choices, are all desirable as responses to depleted natural resources and growing global rates of obesity and chronic disease. A completely hands-off approach in these areas may be a risk factor for future business success.

As Uncle Ben said to Peter Parker in *Spiderman*, "with great power comes great responsibility". Food businesses can use their power to contribute to better health for both people and the planet. As a business leader, you have an enormous capacity to lead change. You can contribute to a food evolution that will help solve food-related problems while also growing market share and enhancing trust and loyalty with your stakeholders. You have the benefits of:

- consistency in investment
- the power to influence
- an understanding of consumer behaviour
- a long-term planning focus
- an in-depth understanding of your food products
- the ability to scale.

Many of the people who work in the business of food are starting to draw on these advantages to make a difference to the future of food as highlighted in the examples provided throughout this book. As someone who works in the industry, you can also make a difference to both population and environmental health, while preparing your business for the future, by adopting purposeful food values that add meaning to your brand.

Part 2 will show you how to do this while Chapter 3 provides additional rationale for adopting a new direction.

A New Approach to Management – The Case for Letting Business Solve Social Problems

In recent years, Michael Porter, Director of the Institute of Strategy and Competitiveness at Harvard Business School, has put forward the case for a new management strategy referred to as 'shared value'. Shared value is a concept that involves companies turning around the perception that business creates social problems and rather, challenges businesses to find opportunities in solving these problems.

Distinct from philanthropy and corporate social responsibility, shared value focuses on a company's ability to maximise the competitive value of solving social problems. This approach enables businesses to build models around achieving social good, in turn differentiating them from their competitors, enhancing their success, enabling talent retention and facilitating cost savings.

According to supporters of this approach, creating shared value is the future for business management.

CHAPTER 3

THE FOOD RE-EVOLUTION

At a conference in New York in 2016, then president and CEO of Campbell Soup Company in the US Denise Morrison, declared, '*The food industry is in a time of revolution.*' No doubt she was right. The shift in sales growth from brands owned by large, traditional food businesses to smaller, 'niche' players indicates how our shopping and eating preferences are changing.

In the US in 2015, small food businesses experienced revenue growth that was almost ten times that of the top 25 food manufacturers — change on a scale not seen since shoppers first migrated to supermarkets in the 1960s. A similar trend is occurring in Australia, with sales data showing big food brands are losing market share to growing boutique, specialist and 'private label' brands.[62] People are now demanding foods that deliver to their changing values, and if traditional food businesses can't provide these options, they are looking elsewhere.

The shift in purchasing habits and rising expectations around what food should deliver are in many ways closer to a re-evolution than a revolution. This is because many of the emerging values that are driving purchasing decisions are linked to elements of the growth, production and consumption of food that were present in the past but that our modern food system dismantled. The further removed we have become from the sources of our food, the more our mistrust has grown. This sense of alienation, in turn, has helped to trigger our need for a closer relationship with food and a closer connection with the people and places responsible for its production.

This re-evolution, reflecting our changing relationship and understanding of food over time, is depicted in figure 3.

Figure 3: The Food Re-evolution

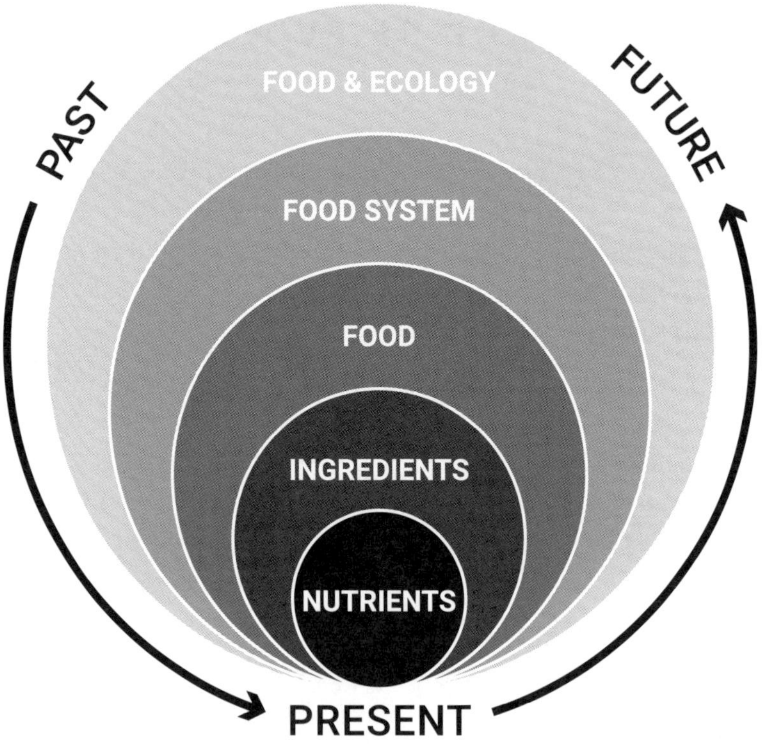

The future lies in the past

Figure 3 conceptualises how our relationship with food has evolved as social and economic factors and technological changes have evolved.

In Neolithic times, hunter-gatherers sourced their food directly from the environment in which they lived. For them, and for the herders and subsistence farmers who followed them, understanding and respecting the interrelationships between food and the environment — from weather to soil to seasonal variations — were necessary survival skills. As human societies evolved over thousands of years, advances in agriculture allowed farmers to obtain greater yields from their crops, until the amount of food produced outpaced rapid population growth. Cities proliferated, rail and road networks enabled the transportation of commodities, including food products, across great distances, and an industrialised food system was developed. But for those living in increasingly urbanised towns and cities, increasing food security and specialised food production meant less direct involvement in growing and producing food. It drove a wedge between many people and the food sources they depended on, and the ancient partnership started to fracture.

Reduced to its parts

Advances in food technology brought new types of food and food processing, longer shelf life, greater variety and more varied flavours. The corner store, which itself had supplanted market stalls, was now replaced by modern supermarkets, with shelf after shelf of enticing, new and colourfully packaged products.

This coincided with the increase in the prevalence of heart disease in the years after the Second World War, captured in emerging results from Ancel Keys' Seven Countries Study[63]. This study demonstrated a link between diet and health, with the finger pointed at fat as a leading risk factor.

As a result, governments started to take note of the influential role of diet in health, introducing dietary guidelines that focused on nutrient content. Food products were scrutinized on ingredients such as fat, salt and sugar content. Food companies started taking a 'for better or for worse' approach to food marketing – changing the composition of food to maximise the positives, such as boosting the fibre content, and to mitigate the negatives, such as reducing the fat content. Marketing teams found new ways to promote foods to an increasingly health-conscious market.

Food technology was responsible for many positive advances, including improvements in food safety, shelf life and accessibility. It also enabled the production of a significantly greater variety of foods, including line extensions that offered more lower fat, reduced sugar, or cholesterol-free options. Over the years, fat, salt and sugar content have remained a key focus in the marketing and development of 'healthier' foods.

Yet today, after decades of 'low-fat', 'diet', 'less sugar' and 'free from' messages, far more people are overweight and obese, type 2 diabetes has risen to epidemic levels, and consumer mistrust of the food industry has only grown. The nutrient-focused approach to food marketing and dietary guideline development, while well intentioned, hasn't contributed to the extent we might have hoped, to reduce diet-related disease.

A blinkered perspective

In my work with food businesses, we have been walking a similar path for years, relying on well worn techniques to communicate the health credentials of food as a key marketing tool. Usual practise is to focus on the end product and to assess its features and benefits. Just as we would look at a car, or a carton of washing powder, the key selling points are identified, such as 'no artificial additives' or 'high in protein', fibre or calcium, or 'low in sugar', salt or saturated fat. These key selling points are highlighted and promoted, while the unwanted ones are ignored. To remain relevant in the future however, this path needs to expand, new tracks need to be explored and the business as usual mindset must be challenged and re-considered as it is clearly no longer generating the results many food businesses are seeking.

Reducing food to the sum of its parts and modifying it to achieve a particular nutritional profile that will in turn make it qualified to be called more nutritious or less harmful, has been driven by a number of factors. These include health related organisations and governments through the establishment of nutrient targets; dietitians educating individuals and the public to look for specific nutritional features of foods; growth in media attention given to nutrition; and schools and universities that teach healthy eating through a nutrient focused lens. Consumer demand for foods that have specific nutritional features has in turn prompted food businesses to develop 'healthier' foods based on modifying their nutritional profile.

Understanding the nutritional value of foods is important, however we are now at a point where it has been over-emphasised while other aspects of food that contribute to its ability to promote and facilitate good health and wellbeing, have been under-emphasised.

Where the food came from, what went into making it and how it is consumed have often not been considered and now this needs to change.

The importance of this in practise is highlighted by Michael Pollan, in his book *In Defense of Food*[52], where he addresses the limitations of a nutrient-based approach to defining food as healthy. He points out that viewing food through this lens assumes it is eaten only for its nutritional considerations. However, this premise is limited and is not shared by all cultures. In particular, a reductionist focus on nutrients overlooks the fact that food may be eaten for other reasons, such as for pleasure or for social identity. These factors do not make people less healthy, and in fact may make them healthier. This point is further supported by Susan Pinker, psychologist, author and social science columnist for The Wall Street Journal mentioned earlier, who outlines how the secret to a longer life may lie in your social life, a great degree of which involves eating together with others.[64]

One of the consequences of focusing on the nutrient profile of foods and modifying foods to achieve specific targets has been that it has led to a significant variety of choices on the market, to the point where the number of products presently available is making it harder for consumers to make effective decisions. It is now clear that we don't need a greater variety of foods – what we really need is more people eating better food. To achieve this, while the nutritional profile of foods will remain one part of the equation, we need to start expanding our view and considering more than this.

From a food marketing perspective, as illustrated in figure 4, simply focusing on nutrients when communicating about a food addresses only 20 per cent of what can be said about it. The opportunity for those in the business of food is therefore to start tapping into the other 80 per cent of what can be said offering significant scope for innovation in marketing and communication. To prepare for the future, taking a broader view that embraces each of the levels outlined — nutrients, ingredients, food, the food system, and food and ecology – will build the foundation for food businesses to have greater future success. This approach will not only meet consumer expectations but also provide significant opportunities to innovate, differentiate and create greater, longer-term consumer engagement.

Figure 4: Opportunities available for food marketing and innovation across the layers of the Food Re-evolution Model

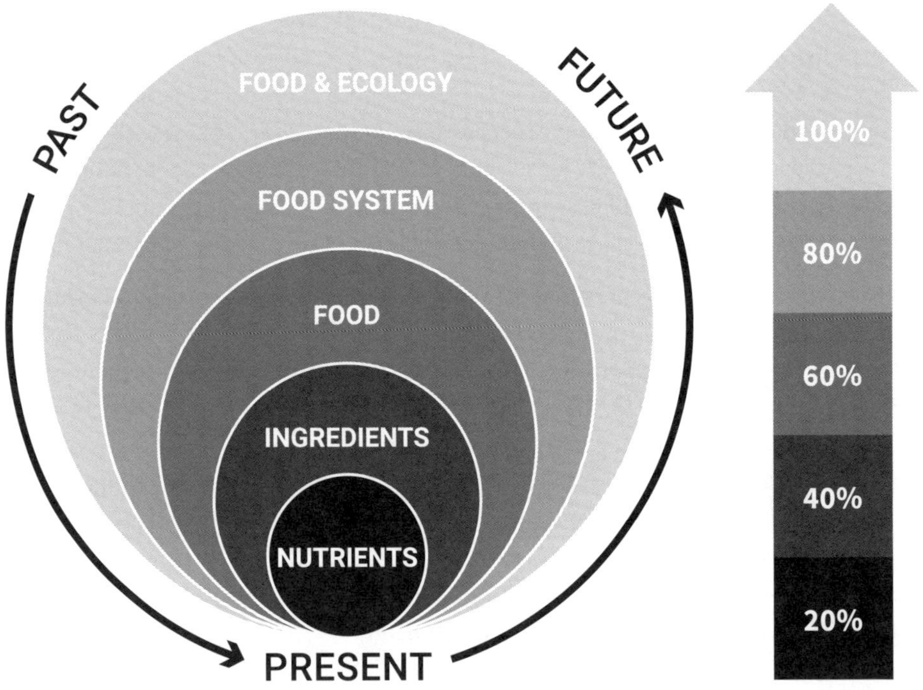

Thinking full circle about food and addressing each of the layers in Figure 4 is a bit like following a recipe. You need all the ingredients to be present and working together to produce an outstanding result.

Nutrition Confusion

As consumer trust in the food supply has been fractured over time, there is now greater scepticism about nutrient focused claims. As a result, focusing too heavily on individual nutrients in food marketing messages can lead to consumer confusion. All areas of the Food Re-evolution Model (figure 4) need to be addressed to create relevancy and to facilitate consistency in positioning. Given that achieving a particular nutritional profile often requires manufacturers to manipulate the ingredients, situations can arise where products making healthy sounding nutrient claims, don't seem to be supported by the ingredient list. Here's one example:

Product: Yoghurt-Coated Muesli Bar.

Claims: Good source of fibre, source of protein, no artificial colours or flavours

Ingredient list: Wholemeal Wheat Flour (Wholemeal Wheat Flour, Wheat Flour, Vitamins (Thiamin, Folate)), Butter (Cream, Water, Salt), Apricot Diced (16%) (Apricot, Rice Flour, Preservative (220)), Yoghurt Compound Coating (11%) (Sugar, Vegetable Oil, Yoghurt Powder (10%), Milk Solids, Emulsifier (Soya Lecithin, 492), Food Acid (330), Brown Sugar, Rolled Oats, Coconut (Coconut, Preservative (220)), Grape Juice Concentrate, Dextrin, Humectant (Glycerine), Baking Powder (450, 500), Natural Flavour, Malic Acid.

From the perspective of the consumer, the impression created by the front of pack nutrient claims may not appear to be supported by the long ingredient list and prevalence of added sugar and additives. This situation can feed consumer mis-trust and uncertainty, while creating inconsistency in brand positioning.

Developing a strategy that crosses all of the layers in the Food Re-evolution Model in Figure 4 offers a comprehensive approach that in turn helps build trust with consumers. It reflects the rising consciousness around the value of food, not just to physical aspects of human health (nutrients), but to many other aspects of our health and wellbeing (ingredients and whole food), and the health and wellbeing of the planet (the food system and the ecological role of food). It satisfies consumer demands by recognising the growing desire to know more about our food and where it comes from. It helps you to differentiate your business by offering multiple combinations of possibilities when forming your strategy. And it creates meaning for your team while helping you to prioritise and plan for the future.

An example of a business addressing each of the layers in the Food Re-evolution Model is Barilla.

Elevating the Link Between Food and Personal and Planetary Health

Barilla has long been a company dedicated to elevating the link between food and both human and planetary health.

In 2010, the Barilla Centre for Food & Nutrition developed the first edition of their 'Double Pyramid'. For the first time, this model recognised that food choices not only needed to be good for human health, but also needed to be good for the long term health of the environment. The Double Pyramid placed both concepts side by side, highlighting the similarities between eating for both personal and planetary health. The graphic depicts a food pyramid on one side and an environmental pyramid on the other. The Double Pyramid has been updated numerous times since and has at it's core the aim of promoting more environmentally sustainable and healthy food choices. It also recognises the role that a proper cultural foundation provides to enable decisions about food to be made and applied on a daily basis, and in a way that reduces the risk of following unbalanced eating patterns. By bringing together experts across various areas of the food system, including those involved in climate change, economics and social health and wellbeing, the Centre is about fostering change toward healthier and more sustainable lifestyles.

This investment in academic work and in providing an avenue for education is consistent with Barilla's vision and values as a business. For further details on Barilla's values, see Chapter 9.

Why tinkering won't work

With the spotlight on health and the social goal of improving our nutritional intake, government and non-government organisations and consumer groups are pressing for more responsible guidelines and codes of practice. In Australia, the Heart Foundation was an initiator with its Tick Program, first introduced in 1989 as a means of encouraging food businesses to reformulate existing products to reduce fat and salt content and offer consumers healthier choices. The recently launched Health Star Rating scheme in Australia and other similar schemes in the UK, US and Europe have the same broad aim: to encourage food businesses to reformulate or develop healthier products.

Taking a nutrient-poor food and tweaking it so it qualifies for a higher star rating, though, is like training for a marathon by walking laps of the oval: it might improve your fitness a little, but it won't be enough to get you past the 5 km mark of the event.

This was highlighted by the critical attention Kellogg's® received when the company reformulated its NutriGrain® product to lift its Star rating from 2 to 4. The reformulated version contained 0.8g more fibre per serve over the original version, 80mg less sodium and the sugar decreased by 2.1g per serve. While these changes are positive, they are small and yet the Star rating doubled. One of the key issues that arose from this reformulation was the concern held by many consumers that the amount of sugar in Nutri-grain® (mostly added sugar) remained high at 26.7%, creating a perceived contrast to its 4 Star rating.

The challenge with reformulation from a business perspective is that companies may risk losing long-term, brand-loyal customers by altering the nutrient profile of well-loved brands and negatively affecting the taste. In 2016, when Arnott's changed the recipe of its iconic Shapes biscuits brand to improve its nutrient profile, the company received significant consumer backlash on its social media pages, along with a 10,000-signature petition to bring back the old Shapes.[65]

Significant planning and resources go into reformulation. Given that changing the recipe of iconic brands poses a high risk for food businesses and the absolute differences achieved are sometimes very small, the impact on public health may be limited. Some, such as the Ministry of Health in Brazil, even think tinkering could make matters worse by taking attention off fresh foods and increasing the focus that is given to more highly processed packaged foods. Focusing on new product development that is driven by a broader set of values that consider the nutritional value of foods alongside other environmental, social and cultural factors provides a whole new range of options for food product development and marketing in the future.

So, while there may be some benefits for some products, reformulation is a small step toward improving public health, however it won't be enough to create significant change and it won't be enough for food businesses looking to accelerate growth and prosper in the future.

An opportunity to lead

Leading in the future will require a significant levelling up. Moving through every layer of the Food Re-evolution Model to take a comprehensive approach to strategy, innovation and marketing will be critical. Future-focused food businesses will not only take this on as a responsibility but will find many new opportunities for business success and growth by referencing this model.

However, doing this alone is still not enough.

There are multiple forces affecting food choices and they are set to continue changing. In the years to come, advances in technology, medical science, artificial intelligence and the internet of things will transform the food we choose, how we eat, whether we preserve cultural and social aspects of our lifestyles and our heritage, how healthy we leave the planet and how healthy we are as a global population. Through the choices made today, food providers have the power to contribute to a more positive future while also creating greater brand differentiation, elevated team engagement and long term, sustainable business growth.

So what else needs to be done? The following chapters provide a direction.

PART 2: VALUES FOR THE FUTURE

'To prosper over time, every company must not only deliver financial performance, but also show how it makes a positive contribution to society.'

Larry Fink, CEO, Blackrock Investments

"Man's search for meaning is the primary motivation in his life and not a 'secondary rationalisation' of instinctual drives.

There are some authors who contend that meanings and values are "nothing but defense mechanisms, reaction formations and sublimations". But as for myself, I would not be willing to live merely for the sake of my "defense mechanisms," nor would I be ready to die merely for the sake of my "reaction formations".

Man, however, is able to live and even to die for the sake of his ideals and values!

We should not, then, be hesitant about challenging man with a potential meaning for him to fulfil.'

Victor Frankl, *Man's Search for Meaning*

CHAPTER 4

THE BENEFITS OF MEANING

Consciousness is building around the way businesses conduct themselves, and this is converging with growing awareness of the impact our lifestyles are having on our personal health and that of the planet. Combined with the impact of technology on social structures and the threatened loss of heritage and culture, the question facing us now is what can food businesses do to prosper in the decades ahead?

The answer may lie in being more meaningful.

Being meaningful is good for business

In 2017, Havas Media Group published the second iteration of their Meaningful Brands Index. In the largest study of its kind, across 33 countries, 300,000 people and 1,500 brands, the research found that brands considered more meaningful outperformed the stock market over a 10-year period (2006–16) by 206 per cent.[2] Meaningful brands also obtained up to nine times the share of wallet and were 137 per cent more likely to meet business key performance indicators, including those related to premium pricing, brand advocacy, brand impression and overall purchases.

These are impressive numbers and provide inspiration for striving toward being more meaningful. So, what does this mean?

The Havas research defined meaningful brands as those that not only meet our functional needs, but also demonstrate an impact on our personal and collective wellbeing. For food brands, functional needs are those related to providing nourishment, satisfying the appetite, providing pleasure or quenching thirst. Demonstrating an impact on personal and collective wellbeing is where meaningful brands distinguish themselves. Another way to look at this is through the lens of demonstrating a social purpose. The finding that people see meaningful brands as those that demonstrate a greater contribution to society, is consistent with the evolution in how people are now expecting companies to operate. According to leaders in the field of corporate strategy, this is one of the most significant opportunities available to businesses today.

In his TED talk in 2013, Michael Porter, Director at the Institute of Strategy and Competitiveness at Harvard Business School, asserted that the opportunity for business to impact social problems was the largest he saw available at that time. He highlighted that a change in thinking was required to move from the conventional wisdom that business profits from causing social problems. Rather, he said, the new thinking is that business profits from solving social problems. The challenge however is to encourage companies to change their thinking.

Five years later, some progress has been made and this concept has infiltrated the mainstream of business. It was reinforced by Larry Fink, CEO of Blackrock Investments, in his annual new year letter to CEOs in January 2018, when he reiterated that brands must not only generate a profit, but also demonstrate a higher social purpose to be relevant to the changing mood of society.

Ken Henry, Chair of the National Australia Bank, also sees the need for businesses to demonstrate a social purpose that drives the way the company operates.[66]

To be authentic, a social purpose needs to be true to the nature of the business and to resonate through the organisation. For food businesses, the opportunity to be genuine and authentic in this space lies in having a social purpose connected to the food you produce. A social purpose centred on your food provides credibility, authenticity, relevance and consistency in positioning over time.

One way to discover and articulate a purpose linked to your food is to develop food centred values — beliefs you hold about your food and the role it plays in the lives of your customers, stakeholders, community, suppliers and employees, and how it impacts the environment in which you operate.

Having food values is also one way to create brand trust.

Stacey Bingle, Consumer Trends Consultant at Mintel, recently highlighted that the number one lesson for businesses seeking to create brand trust is to state their values. Today it's clear that if you're not defining yourself on social values as a business, someone else will do it for you. Building trust by stating your values is a key way forward for food businesses.

Figure 5 shows the benefits of food values, compared to corporate and consumer values, when it comes to developing brand meaning. The y axis plots meaningfulness, a measure that is associated with the achievement of key business performance indicators; the x axis shows the three types of values food companies may adopt. All are important; however, adding food values to the usual corporate and consumer values provides a way of elevating meaningfulness, driving business performance and differentiating your brand.

Figure 5: The journey from 'me too' to meaningful

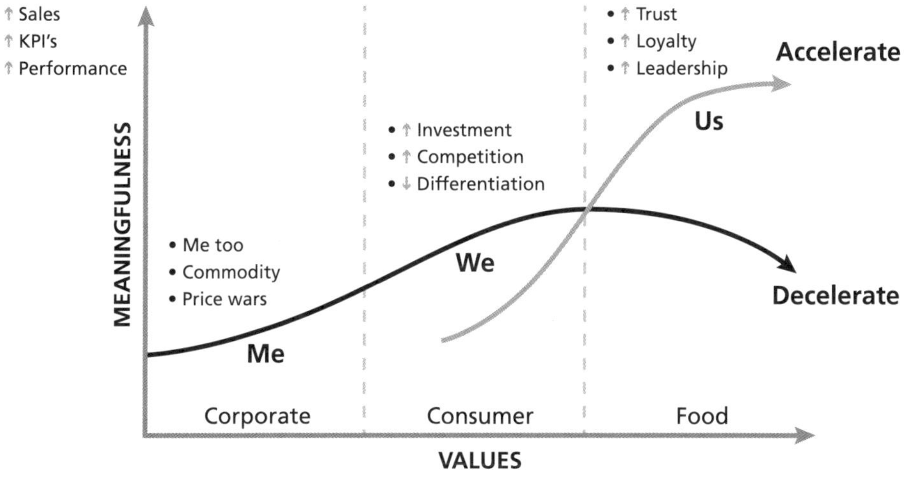

From 'me too' to meaningful

Figure 5 outlines the three types of values that food businesses can create and adopt to guide internal decision making, strategy and brand positioning. The following section unpacks this model and clarifies the three categories of values, outlining why the development of values that are specifically centred on the food that a business produces is a key strategy for future relevance as it provides a way of demonstrating social purpose and creating a higher level of brand meaning.

Level 1: Corporate values alone

For any business, the price of entry to performing effectively in the market is to develop corporate values. Corporate values are statements about what a business believes are important in order to create the results it seeks. Typical corporate values could relate to teamwork, innovation, customer service, performance, respect and efficiency. These values are implemented throughout the business by taking actions that support them. For example, if a corporate value is loyalty, and a new position comes up within the organisation, it would be reasonable to expect that the person who had been with the company for 25 years would be offered the opportunity over someone who had been there for only a year.

Corporate values are internally focused. They guide internal workings and culture and therefore have a 'me' focus — they are about *my* company or *my* business. As corporate values have an internal focus, they generally create little direct meaning for consumers. In today's changing environment, and for those looking to engage with the evolving and more mindful consumer, a broader set of values that can be shared with consumers is required.

Level 2: Corporate and consumer values

Most food businesses invest in understanding consumer values to assist in tailoring and developing products that meet the needs of the market. Often a usage and attitudes survey will be done, and the results used to guide strategy. Asking the market what they want and delivering this is basic marketing practice — find out and then give the customer what they are seeking. In this area the focus turns from 'me' to 'we'. Most food businesses sit in this area.

Those who lead in their ability to respond to consumer trends have the advantage of being first to market. However, even with this advantage, they can find that if they remain too long with one new product concept, the competition catches up, and it's imperative to continue innovating. Starting out with a differentiated offering that is soon copied by competitors means it can get crowded in this space. Investment in innovation is constantly required. If innovation is based on tweaks to existing products, this can lead to an overabundance of brands and choices and a highly cluttered market, leading to significant competition for shelf space.

Similarly, manufacturers and food service businesses may find an increase in inefficiencies arising as a result of the need to maintain a diversity of products or menu offerings developed in response to consumer demand. For manufacturers, the need to add new lines to accommodate more and more new products can lead to reduced productivity in the factory. Time is lost with the increasing frequency with which equipment needs to be cleaned and lines switched over to accommodate each new product that is introduced.

An additional challenge here is that consumer values are constantly changing. This means marketing and innovation efforts consistently need to adapt to keep up with the latest trends and remain relevant. Ongoing re-investment can be expensive and lead to a cluttered market. Without this investment however there is a risk that sales growth will decelerate.

Level 3: Food values

Creating food values provides a means of accelerating growth and lifting a company or brand from a 'me too' position to one that is more meaningful. Food values are statements about what a company believes about the food it produces. They address beliefs about the nutritional profile of the products, ingredients used, production, packaging, consumption, and social and cultural aspects. When these values are clear and translated into commitments and actions, they have significant benefits that flow through many aspects of the business. These include greater team agility and the ability to make quicker and better decisions. Rather than adjusting decisions according to changes in consumer opinion or the activity of competitors, decisions are driven by the beliefs held about the role brands play in the lives of customers and stakeholders, in communities and in the environment. By standing for something bigger than the end product produced, businesses create greater meaning behind their brand. This ultimately leads to better long-term business performance. As outlined earlier, meaningful brands outperform the stock market by more than double over a 10 year period. They also gain up to 9 times share of a consumer's wallet and are 137% more likely to meet business key performance indicators (KPI's).

Once you have developed your food values (and the next chapter will show you how to do this step by step), you have content through which you can communicate in a more meaningful way with consumers.

Your food values put you in a position to influence consumer opinion, to showcase your expertise and then build your reputation in areas that complement your business. Your commitments outline what you are going to do to bring these values to life.

Chapters 5 and 6 take you through the development of your food-focused values, while chapter 7 provides guidance on leveraging these values to develop your voice in the market.

'If you're not consistent in the things you say and do, no-one will know what you believe.'

Simon Sinek

CHAPTER 5

THE FOOD VALUES MODEL

Creating food centred values provides a critical connection point between you and your customers and stakeholders. These values are developed by drawing from both your corporate values and consumer values. When they are clear, food centred values enable you to make quicker and better decisions, to create consistency in your communication and marketing and to stand for something bigger than the end products you sell. Rather than adjusting decisions according to changes in consumer opinion or the activity of competitors, decisions are driven by the beliefs held about the role your food plays in the lives of your customers, communities, environment and stakeholders.

The model below illustrates how food centred values provide a filter through which to make decisions that both complement consumer and corporate values while also building trust and enabling meaningful connections to occur.

Figure 6: Food Values Model

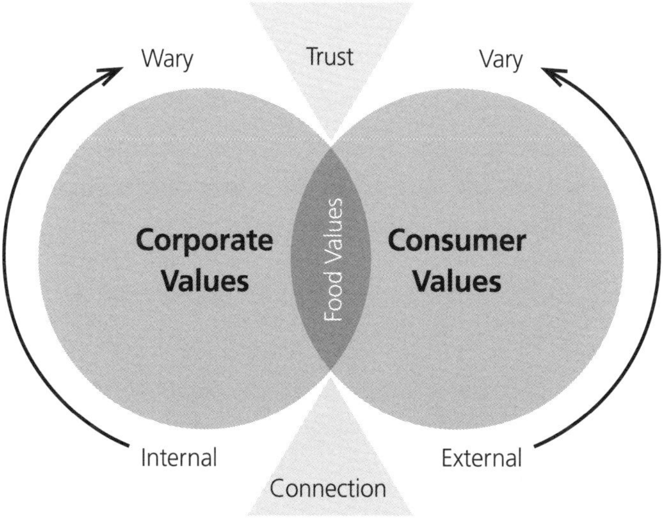

As mentioned in chapter 4, it's likely you have corporate values in place for your business (left hand side of figure 6), and also that you spend some of your time and money investing in consumer research to find out what consumers value when it comes to food purchasing and selection (right hand side of figure 6).

Corporate values however are internally focused and in general aren't communicated externally. Rather, they guide internal culture and behaviours. If communicated to consumers, corporate values can risk having them feel wary. For example, values such as ambition, productivity and efficiency can alienate consumers as they increasingly look to business to demonstrate a greater social purpose.

Consumer values on the other hand are externally focused. They are the values consumers look for when it comes to their food purchasing decisions. The downside of simply following consumer values is that they vary over time. This increases the investment your business needs to make in market research and innovation to stay relevant.

Food values (middle of figure 6) are different from corporate values, and from consumer values, while taking both into account. They are not based on driving profit, although working with a set of guiding values around your food will ultimately benefit your bottom line. Food values are also not completely driven by what consumers say they value, although they are likely to reflect that. Rather, they outline what you believe about your products, your portfolio, the role your food plays in enhancing people's lives, and the health of the planet — the bigger picture issues you value as a company and around which you feel inspired to make a difference. Food values have a strong influence on consumer perceptions about your brand.

Your food values, backed up with a clear set of commitments and actions, will help put your business in a position that enables you to develop your customers' trust and long-term loyalty, while also enhancing the meaning of your brand. They provide a greater sense of purpose, facilitating engagement with your team and stakeholders. And they enable you to make leadership decisions efficiently and effectively.

There are different ways to go about developing your food values. One simple approach is to review your corporate values, and where applicable translate these into food centred values. You can then cross-check these against what you know about consumer values. Table 5 offers some examples.

Table 5: Simple approach to developing your food values

Example of corporate value	Translated into a food centred value	Cross-checked against consumer values
Customer service	Our food contributes to making our customers' lives healthier.	Health and wellbeing
Teamwork	Our food serves to bring people together.	Social aspects of eating
Ambition	In developing our food, we do all we can to maximise and preserve its natural nutritional goodness.	Natural
Integrity	We always communicate accurately and truthfully about the way our food is produced and where it comes from.	Transparency and honesty
Innovation	We strive to find new ways to help people improve their health through food.	New food experiences
Productivity	Our food is produced in a way that minimises our use of natural resources.	Responsible production

This approach provides a quick and simple starting point. It helps you see how existing corporate values lend themselves to supporting food centred values, and in turn gives you confidence around consistency of operations. It also provides an umbrella for a future focused strategy. If you feel you need to go deeper, the rest of this chapter outlines a more comprehensive and thorough approach to developing your food values.

This process aims at extending your thinking beyond the everyday business-as-usual to a broader, bigger-picture perspective. It has you take on a role within the environment in which you operate to proactively lead the way to a better future through the food you make, how you make it and what you stand for. It demonstrates how you and your business are committed to making a difference to the world in which you operate.

It's useful to think of food values as falling into four key domains, as outlined in figure 7. By having values in each of these areas you are encompassing the elements that contribute to the development of a comprehensive food values charter. The bottom section of the model (internal) is more closely linked with consumer values and corporate values. These are areas you create – you create your products; their ingredients and formulation and you are responsible for creating your business culture. The top two sections (external) are where you can really start to differentiate your brand. These are areas that you can influence. They're not values that you find in the marketplace and respond to, or that necessarily exist right now within your business, but rather values you, your team and your business believe in. To articulate values in these areas you may need to draw on external advisors and experts to guide you.

Figure 7: Key segments of a food values charter

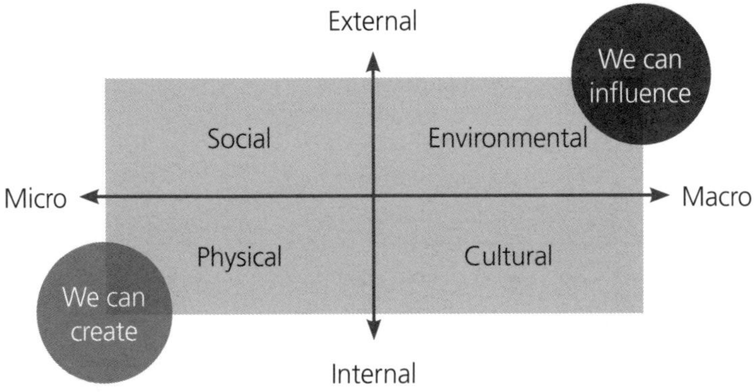

The following provides an additional explanation around each segment:

Physical. The physical attributes of your products include their nutritional profile, the ingredients used, and elements that contribute to consumers' safety concerns, such as the presence or absence of allergens or particular substances, or methods of processing. Physical attributes of your products are what most marketers and innovators will focus on. It is an area you likely feel comfortable addressing. It's most closely linked to consumer values and is often driven by what you know about your market and the technology you use to produce your products. For example, many companies may have nutrient targets, or guidelines around the use of particular ingredients, that fit into this section.

Cultural. The cultural aspects of your values will reflect the heritage and history of your company and the cultural aspects of the products you sell. For example, your business may have started as an Italian family business with strong cultural links to this cuisine. Or it could be that you have particular expertise in a process such as baking or fermentation, or in a food type such as dairy foods or grains. The cultural element of your food values has the strongest link to your corporate values.

Social. The social attributes of your products and your approach to marketing include the frequency and types of messages used in the communication about your products, how your products may enhance your customers' lives socially, and whether you believe you have a role to play in educating your customers. When it comes to the social aspects of food and its role in our lives, you are guided by what you believe in. Social considerations are often less likely to be addressed by food businesses, so you may benefit from some external facilitation to assist you to develop meaningful values in this area.

Environmental. Environmental aspects of your products include the way they are produced, the packaging used and the way you communicate how they are to be consumed. Initiatives in this area may be influenced by regulations around environmental compliance, so the key question is whether you feel you have a role over and above these regulations. Here you can draw on your own internal beliefs about how you feel your company should operate within the broader context of environmental stewardship from both a production and consumption viewpoint.

The Food Values Wheel shown in Figure 8 takes the four categories within which food values can be developed and splits them into sub-categories. These sub-categories provide a starting point for guiding the development of your specific food centred values. Questions relevant to each segment that will help you unveil your food values are outlined in the following section. Time to work on the detail!

Figure 8: The Food Values Wheel

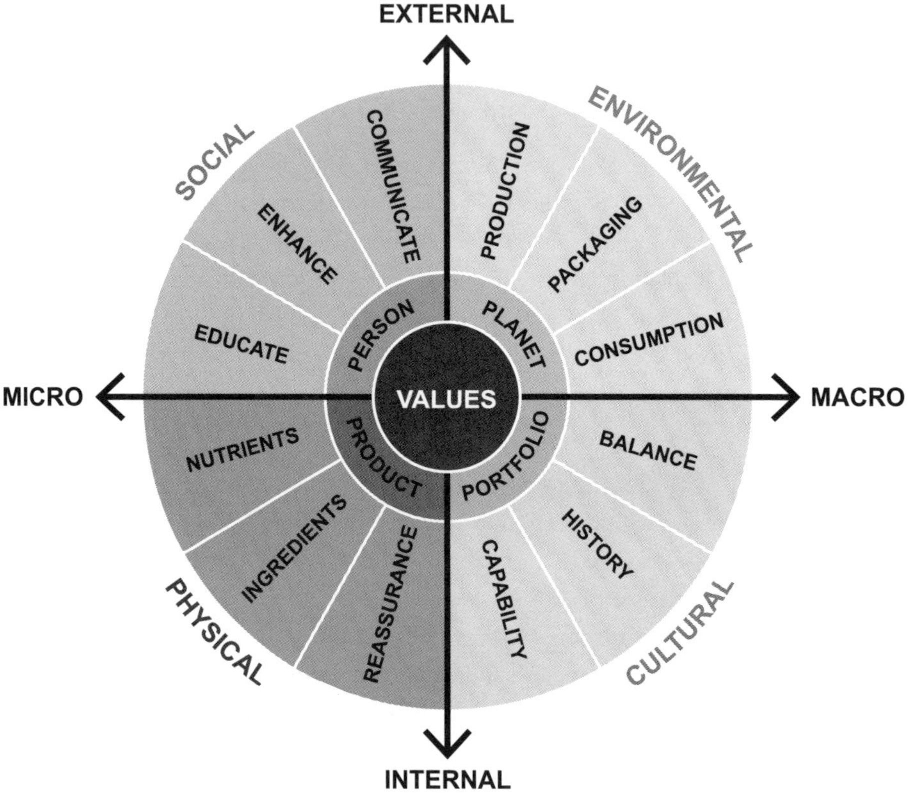

Develop Your Food Centred Values

This section outlines a detailed process for getting started on the path to creating greater meaning for your business, products and brands through the development of food centred values.

The first step is to audit where you are at and to define what is important to you. The second step is to review, and the third step is to create. After that, we will get to the point of developing your commitments and then to putting your values to work for you.

Step 1: Audit

This first round of questions requires you simply to answer yes or no. Where you answer no, the next question asks whether this is something that would be valuable for your business to have. This process helps create a thorough set of food values which in turn will be more meaningful.

Physical

- Do you have benchmark nutrient criteria against which you evaluate your portfolio of products?

Yes ☐ No ☐
↓
Would this be of value to your business? Yes ☐ No ☐

- Do you have standards against which you select ingredients or preferred suppliers?

Yes ☐ No ☐
↓
Would this be of value to your business? Yes ☐ No ☐

- Do you have a list of ingredients, additives or by-products that you will not include in any of your products?

Yes ☐ No ☐
↓
Would this be of value to your business? Yes ☐ No ☐

Social

- Do you have guidelines around the way you communicate that demonstrate you understand the positive social effects of food?

Yes ☐ No ☐
↓
Would this be of value to your business? Yes ☐ No ☐

- Do you have in place any initiatives or commitments around helping your customers/others to live a healthy lifestyle or to make healthier eating easier?

Yes ☐ No ☐
↓
Would this be of value to your business? Yes ☐ No ☐

- Do you undertake any activities to educate consumers/your customers?

Yes ☐ No ☐
↓
Would this be of value to your business? Yes ☐ No ☐

Cultural

- Do you have any targets around the balance of products you offer across your portfolio?

Yes ☐ No ☐
↓
Would this be of value to your business? Yes ☐ No ☐

- Does your portfolio include products that have a historical significance or a strong cultural connection?

Yes ☐ No ☐
↓
Would this be of value to your business to develop? Yes ☐ No ☐

- Do you have expertise in a technology, food type, packaging or other area that sets you apart?

Yes ☐ No ☐
↓
Would this be of value to your business to develop or highlight? Yes ☐ No ☐

Environmental

- Do you have any commitments in place around the environmental impact of your production processes?

Yes ☐ No ☐
↓
Would this be of value to your business? Yes ☐ No ☐

- Do you have any commitments in place around the environmental impact of your packaging?

Yes ☐ No ☐
↓
Would this be of value to your business? Yes ☐ No ☐

- Do you have any commitments around promoting responsible consumption and minimising waste and overconsumption?

Yes ☐ No ☐
↓
Would this be of value to your business? Yes ☐ No ☐

Step 2: Review

For all the questions to which you ticked yes, identify/describe this commitment.

Then complete the following sentence:

We have this commitment in place because:

Then answer this question:

What value does this demonstrate?

Example:

If you already have commitments in place that relate to the nutritional value of your products, you may have something like this:

Our benchmark nutrient criteria include:

Our meals will provide a maximum of 30 per cent of the daily intake for energy.

We have this commitment in place because: we understand that weight gain is a significant risk factor for long-term health and quality of life. We value the health of our customers and have put this initiative in place because we feel a responsibility to serve them well.

What value does this demonstrate?

This demonstrates we value our customers' health and wellbeing.

Now you can summarise this in a statement for inclusion in a food values charter for your business. In this case, this value could be written as:

We value our customers' health and wellbeing.

Step 3: Create

Review the answers to the questions to which you answered 'no' then ticked 'yes'. These are the areas you have identified as of value to your business and therefore worth working on. You will need to brainstorm actions and commitments to demonstrate your values in these areas.

Example:

You have identified that you don't have any commitments around promoting responsible consumption or minimising food waste. This would be of value to your business as you understand your customers are taking a greater level of interest in both areas.

Brainstorm: What could we do?

We could:

- decide to take a stand against upselling offers that encourage people to buy more than they need
- clearly identify on our packaging what one serving is
- encourage people to make our food go further by providing examples
- provide containers to encourage taking home leftovers
- encourage consumers to reuse the packaging our products come in
- introduce steps in the production process that reduce the amount of food wasted
- undertake research with our suppliers to source ingredients that are made from food that would otherwise be wasted.

From this list, priorities can be selected, and commitments made.

Step 4: Commit

Once you have established your core values, these need to be translated into commitments and, most important, actions. This is of course an essential step, because without actions, your food values risk being no more than empty claims on a wall poster, which can be demotivating for your team and contribute to indifference over the long term.

It is also important to have confidence that your values can be executed with consistency and integrity. Your team needs to be on board and understand and own what you stand for, so it can be accurately translated through all relevant areas of your business. So, it's important only to commit to actions that can be implemented. At the same time, any commitment that's working toward a better future needs to stretch your business too. It's a matter of finding the balance between positively moving forward and creating the possibility of something bigger. Just like a long road trip, to manage driver fatigue, sometimes you will need to take a break and reset before beginning the next leg of the journey. The next chapter provides some ideas for action aimed at stimulating your thinking.

CHAPTER 6

SETTING COMMITMENTS

Now you have developed your values, your commitments and actions will follow and will demonstrate how you will be putting your values into practice. Your commitments and actions will likely form part of your overall strategy for marketing, operations, research and development, and innovation. As mentioned, start with commitments you are confident you can fulfil and build from there.

If your business lacks an in-depth understanding of the four areas that go into creating your values, it will be more challenging to develop commitments that are grounded in good science and are authentic. Yet this is critical if your food values are to have longevity. To help, this chapter provides some thought starters, based on the Food Values Wheel's four main values classes, to set you on the right path toward embodying the spirit of 'food for a better future' and to creating greater brand meaning. Not all of these ideas will be relevant to your situation, but they provide a menu from which you can choose those that will be most useful for you. You may also call on external advisers to assist and facilitate this process.

Physical

Nutrients

Governments are focusing increasingly on the role food providers play in relation to public health issues, notably around overweight and obesity and associated lifestyle-related diseases and are increasingly putting in place regulations and guidelines around the nutritional value of food to qualify for point-of-sale symbols or to be approved for sale in various outlets such as school canteens. While this nutrient focused approach has its limitations, as outlined in chapter 3, it is necessary to address this area if you want your products to be available for sale through certain outlets. The nutritional profile of products is also important if you are targeting a particular market for a specific health benefit or you currently have products that are quite low in nutritional value.

Nutrient targets can be set to support values around product improvements, or to ensure a therapeutic benefit for a particular target group. Examples include:

- setting targets to reduce added sodium, saturated fat or added sugar within a specified period of time
- setting targets to increase fibre, protein, vitamins or minerals within a particular product range and within a specified period of time.
- setting a goal of having the nutritional profile of products tested and using this information consistently in consumer communications and education.

Ingredients

Coming out of the low-fat era, when population rates of overweight and obesity continued to grow, and consumer opinion turned to 'you took the fat out but added more sugar', nutrient claims on their own are now less likely to be believed without also checking the ingredient list. The trend toward 'clean labelling' has been in response to the desire to avoid additives and anything artificial. Targets that can be set around ingredients include:

- sourcing only locally or ethically produced ingredients
- using ingredients that support local or small hold farmers or communities.
- using only ingredients derived from natural whole foods
- setting targets to eliminate certain additives or ingredients
- setting targets around the way ingredients are prepared, produced or grown.

Reassurance

Reassurance about your product will be derived from your ability to demonstrate that it is safe and free from allergens or other substances your consumers or main target group are looking to avoid. It can also include commitments linked to animal or soil welfare. Targets in this area might include a commitment to:

- zero trans fats, acrylamide or ingredients derived from genetically modified crops
- sustainable sourcing
- no pesticide residues, hormones or antibiotics.

Note: Take care that you are committing to issues that are scientifically sound, as well as relevant and important to your business. You may need additional expert input in this area to avoid making commitments based on what's in trend but not scientifically supported.

Social

Educate

You may have decided you want to take a more influential role to develop values around educating your consumers in areas of relevance to your products. This picks up on consumers' increasing desire for more food-related experiences. A value relating to education could be linked to helping people to improve their eating habits or to learn a new skill relevant to your product range. It might also be aimed at raising awareness about why a particular ingredient, an additive for example, is used in your products.

Examples of commitments in this area include:

- educating consumers about how your product is made
- demonstrating techniques that are used when making your product that consumers can use at home, for example, how to ferment or preserve food
- running classes or workshops on areas of relevance to your product range (cooking or food preparation skills, for example, or how to reduce food waste)
- teaching children how to cook, garden or understand where food comes from, and how it is grown, processed and packaged.

Enhance

You may believe your company is well placed to take a leadership position that enables you to enhance the lives of your customers and other stakeholders (such as suppliers and employees). Enhancing lives can be about making it easy for people to adopt healthy lifestyle habits, supporting local community initiatives, helping address larger global issues, or helping people to reduce stress and gain more control in their lives.

Examples of commitments in this area include:

- contributing a portion of sales to a food- or health-related charity, synergistic with your product range
- committing to supporting food related initiatives in the local community in which your business operates
- creating a foundation that's meaningful to your business
- enhancing people's experiences with food (for example, through diverse new flavours, ethnic cuisines, ingredients that support biodiversity or the use of indigenous ingredients)

- supporting initiatives that address global food related issues such as food waste, hunger, biodiversity or agroecology
- committing to a healthy workplace
- helping your suppliers to improve their products

Connect

One of the down sides of the way technology has infiltrated our lives is that in some cases, it has reduced the time we spend connecting with people in real time, face to face. Food is a great connector. If the way your food is consumed matters to you, you may believe you can play a role to encourage social connections through the way you advertise your food — for example, as best enjoyed when shared with others, or as a gift idea, or through creating recipes that connect people to particular cuisines.

Connection is also about how you connect with your consumers. For example, you might commit not to advertise to children under a certain age, or not to use particular outlets or modes of advertising while supporting others.

Examples of commitments in this area include:

- always showing people eating together when advertising your food
- adopting messages to encourage people to share your food
- never showing people eating while doing something else, such as driving or using a mobile phone
- supporting the gift-giving aspects of your food (for example, by encouraging people to share and gift it on special occasions)
- not advertising your food products in contexts that promote overconsumption

Cultural

Balance

Balance is about the breadth of products in your range, on your menu or within a particular brand portfolio. Mintel, in their 2018 Asia Pacific consumer trends research, found consumers are increasingly feeling overwhelmed by the wide abundance of options on offer and in his book *The Paradox of Choice*, Barry Schwartz explains that too much choice makes it harder for people to choose. How much is enough, though? Offering sufficient variety to achieve what you value is the key to reflecting and developing your commitments in this area.

Examples of potential commitments include:

- deciding on the percentage of your product range that will meet certain health-related criteria.
- offering products in different portion sizes (small, medium and large) - in particular, ensuring there is a smaller portion size available
- providing choice for people with differing health needs
- offering a maximum but limited number of choices overall.

Capability

What you produce and how you communicate about your products and services will reflect your capabilities. You may be satisfied with the degree to which your capabilities enable you to operate within your market, or you may have values around improving them to realise bigger or different goals or objectives.

Examples of commitments in this area include:

- valuing your internal expertise
- elevating the voice of internal experts
- committing to complementing your own expertise with that of external experts such as nutritionists, chefs, farmers, environmental scientists, nutrition researchers or technologists
- building your capabilities to improve the nutritional value of your products
- building your capabilities to reduce your environmental impact

History

History here relates to the history of your business, your products or the background of your key people — that is, the elements of your business that have significantly influenced the way you operate and what you hold to be important. Values in this area will often provide a unique element to your food charter. Historical elements can relate to your original aims when developing your first products, the way they have been produced or the sourcing of the ingredients. Tapping into the heritage of your food can be one of the keys to differentiation, demonstrating integrity and gaining the trust of consumers.

Examples of commitments in this area include:

- standing behind the formula of your heritage products and not tampering with them
- always sourcing ingredients in a way that maintains the historical integrity of your products
- remaining true to the cultural traditions behind your products
- honouring your past while innovating to prepare for the future.
- using heirloom ingredients

Environmental

Production

Food production contributes significantly to human impact on the environment and finding ways to reduce this impact is critical for the long term health of the planet. Initiatives in this area will also assist countries meet the UN Sustainable Development Goals given food production accounts for 30 percent of the world's total energy consumption and 22 percent of Greenhouse Gas emissions. To make a difference, perhaps you want to develop values around the responsible use of water, materials or land, or around resource-efficient transportation and distribution.

Examples of commitments in this area include:

- using recycled water throughout your production plant
- favouring more local ingredients to reduce the amount of energy used in distribution
- supporting indigenous cultures and communities by using their materials or ingredients that are naturally adapted to the local environment
- working with suppliers who employ technologies that assist farmers with efficiencies to get 'more from less' or to grow food in a way that has a lower impact on the environment
- reducing food waste throughout the production system
- using ingredients and processes that support biodiversity.

Packaging

Another of the key contributors to the environmental impact of food production is packaging. This has been highlighted by the recent consumer backlash against retailers who use too much packaging when selling fresh produce and initiatives such as 'Nude Food Day', when children are encouraged to bring to school only food and food products that involve no packaging.

Examples of commitments in this area include:

- lightening your packaging to reduce the use of raw materials
- educating customers about recycling or reusing packaging
- reducing packaging such as lids, bags or other containers for carrying products after purchase
- limiting or discouraging use of plastic wrapping, straws or utensils.

Consumption

Food makers have been criticised for encouraging overconsumption of food when this has been counterproductive to health and the environment. In her book *Food Politics*, public health nutritionist Marion Nestle reviews the food industry's history of 'eat more' messaging and the tendency to push back on any initiatives that encourage consumers to 'eat less'. Industry leaders today are beginning to recognise that a responsibility to the health of both the consumer and the environment is part of being a conscious and therefore more sustainable business.

Examples of commitments in this area include:

- responsibly promoting appropriate portion sizes
- offering smaller portion sizes
- educating around eating strategies that help reduce overconsumption
- taking a stand against two-for-one type deals that may promote overconsumption
- discouraging people from overeating by downsizing crockery and cups used to serve food
- avoiding or minimising the use of words such as 'massive', 'stuffed' or 'mega' in advertising and promotion.

With your food values in place, the next step is to develop them into an overall philosophy or charter (refer back to page 78 for how to do this). Once this is clear, you will be ready to communicate this throughout your business, ensuring all staff embrace and understand their role in realising your food values and the associated commitments. To achieve these commitments, you may need to establish new processes, procedures, suppliers, messages and standards. There are likely many flow through effects and actions that will need to be addressed. Over time, among the rewards for your effort however, will be the ability to make quicker decisions more effectively, to create greater team engagement, and to enhance consumer loyalty and trust.

Table 6 shows examples of food values and philosophies that have been adopted successfully by a range of food businesses. These are top-line values that are frequently communicated to the public to highlight the key values of the company around the production and marketing of their food products.

Le Pain Quotidien – An Excerpt from the Company's Food Philosophy

At Le Pain Quotidien, we believe that community is what nurtures, inspires and feeds the soul.

Our tables are where friends re-connect and new friendships are forged over the shared appreciation of delicious food and good company.

In a space where colour comes to life, music mingles with the melody of conversation and fresh-baked smells stoke the imagination, there will always be a place for you at our table.

Table 6: Examples of purposeful food values attested to by particular food companies

Business	Elements of company's food values
Danone	'Bringing health through food to as many people as possible'
Harris Farm	'We're for the greater goodness.' 'We've believed in something greater than just selling fresh food. We've believed in nature itself. Which is why we're doing our best to make it all it can be.'
Next Door	'We are committed to real food from American farmers. We know where our food comes from.'
Chobani	'We believe in better food for more people.'
Mars Food	'Food should be an experience.' 'Great food is both science and art.' 'Our food should make life easier.'
Barilla	'Good for you, good for the planet'
Sweet Earth Natural Foods	'Honour and sustain the land.' 'Cultivate a curious mind and palate.' 'Sustain a healthy body.'
Grill'd Healthy Burgers	'Made with love' 'Burgers done good.' 'Be good. Do good. Feel good.'
Whole Foods Market	'We sell the highest quality natural and organic foods.' 'We satisfy, nourish and delight our customers.' 'We promote the health of our stakeholders through healthy eating education.'
Laneway Greens	'We believe less hands make honest food.'

Now your values are in place, the next critical step is communicating these to the market and to key stakeholders. Chapter 7 provides guidance in this area to ensure your values come through in a genuine and authentic way and the benefits of your investment in this process are realised.

'As you live your values, your sense of identity, integrity, control, and inner-directedness will infuse you with both exhilaration and peace. You will define yourself from within, rather than by people's opinions or by comparisons to others'.

Stephen Covey

PART 3: A VOICE TO LEAD THE FUTURE

'Our lives begin to end the day we become silent about things that matter.'

Martin Luther King, Jr.

'When you build an audience you don't have to buy people's attention - they give it to you'.

Jason Fried

CHAPTER 7

INSPIRING ATTENTION

Information about food is available 24/7. We can check facts, find answers, seek other's opinions and share our thoughts with the world in an instant. Public access to information about food has increased enormously through technology, but while this can be helpful, it can also lead to confusion. When suspicion is raised about what's in food, or how it is made, the news can spread like wildfire, quickly turning from myth to reality and creating unwanted and unexpected consequences for food businesses. If concerns escalate significantly, they can lead to the need to react to defend yourself, taking what can be unnecessary actions that distract you from getting on with business. Being on the defensive is, of course, not as powerful or effective as being on the offensive.

One example was the issue of permeate being added to milk. As a result of media reporting, consumer concern was raised about milk producers adding permeate to their milk prior to packaging.

Permeate is the by-product of dairy food production and consists of lactose, vitamins and minerals. It is sometimes used to standardise the fat and protein levels in milk to assist in delivering a consistent end product. The use of permeate in milk generated headlines a few years ago about milk producers watering down their milk with the implication being they were 'ripping people off'. Without the industry sharing its specific knowledge earlier about how milk was made and why various parts of the milk may be added or removed prior to packaging, the situation resulted in many dairy companies reacting by changing their packaging to include claims that it was 'permeate free'. While this appeased the vocal minority, the silent majority hadn't heard of permeate prior to the words appearing on packaging and it became a point of further confusion for many, rather than a point that enabled producers to gain a competitive advantage. These claims have since been removed from most milk cartons in Australia - a costly exercise to defend a lack of understanding.

With evolving consumer values demanding more information about food, those responsible for growing, making, marketing and selling food will benefit from being part of the narrative. It is no longer smart to remain silent about how food is made, what's in it and its role in a balanced and sustainable diet. It is critical to have a bigger share of voice in the market. Greater transparency and a greater level of expertise that is shared with the market will provide a useful platform for those looking to remain in business over the long-term.

Stand on Your Milk Crate

Establishing food centred values provides clarity about what you stand for and provides a meaningful foundation from which to communicate and act. Your food values are the milk crate on which you can stand to speak out – they serve to elevate your voice. Written up into a charter or philosophy, they provide the context around what you believe while your commitments outline what you are going to do to bring these values to life. With these elements in place, you are ready to communicate with your market in a way that inspires their attention and builds their trust. Communicating out to the market is a critical third step in the process.

Some have started to take this on. Danone's strategy around 'One Planet. One Health' includes a commitment to increasing transparency. They have distributed short videos on social media in which their internal experts talk about the farmers they work with, the sustainability commitments and projects they have in various countries, and other activities and projects they are engaged in.

Brasserie Bread have developed in-person educational programs and videos showing people how to bake bread. They are passionate about sharing their knowledge as bakers, and to pass on their expertise. Their baking classes are now attended by hundreds of school students annually. Investing in this program is congruent with who they are as a business. More farmers, artisans and chefs are also having a voice around how food is grown, prepared and cooked. This more open and transparent approach, where companies and their suppliers are communicators and educators is a key way forward.

Raising the profile of your experts and giving them the confidence to talk knowledgeably about your products and processes, has the carry-over effect of empowering team members, making them feel valued and generating greater loyalty. Their expertise also gives consumers confidence that can help generate trust. Ultimately this is of significant business value over the long term.

Getting Noticed

In my experience working with food businesses over the years there is often a great deal of expertise and passion that sits behind products and brands but goes unseen by the public. A failure to share more about food production, the challenges food producers face and to take responsibility for educating the public on relevant food related issues has created a void that has been filled with other voices, such as those of public health officials, government, bloggers or self-proclaimed experts on social media. This is one factor that has likely contributed to low levels of trust in the food system and created widespread cynicism toward food manufacturers. The food industry, producers and growers have either not put forward an effective voice, been overlooked by the media and advertisers, or perhaps haven't built the foundation on which to base messages that resonate with consumers in a genuine and authentic way.

It's important to be clear, however, that the goal is not to create a voice simply to add noise in the market. As noted earlier, every day some 500 million tweets, 4.3 billion Facebook messages and 500 million hours of YouTube footage are sent, posted or uploaded. We are swamped by information and interruptions, and this is creating stress and a sense of overwhelm. Rather, the goal is to inspire attention and draw people to your brand or business. Pairing the messages that reflect your values with spokespeople who believe in what you stand for is the pathway to achieving this.

Finding your voice

To develop a voice that effectively communicates your values and draws people toward your brand or product it is essential to carefully select the spokespeople you use. In the past, as still today, marketers have often drawn on celebrities, sportspeople, models or external experts as the voice of their brands. This was the case when I worked for a major food producer in the early 1990s. At this time the company was heavily involved in a high profile sporting event held as a series in various locations in Australia and New Zealand. The competitors, along with one of Australia's most successful swimmers, were regularly used as spokespeople for the brand. This was a highly effective marketing campaign at the time, as many of the company's products were considered healthy and a good fit with Australian sport. Today, however, muesli bars, one of the companies staple products, are categorised as a 'discretionary food' in the government's Australian Guide to Healthy Eating, meaning they are a food considered suitable only for occasional, rather than daily, consumption. This is in contrast to how muesli bars were viewed in the 1990s and highlights how our understanding and attitudes can change over the years.

Similarly, with consumers becoming more sceptical of food marketers' claims and demanding greater levels of transparency, the use of external voices to communicate a company's food centred values can often be less effective than an expert from within the business. To create authenticity and trust through communications, using real people is now considered more effective than relying on celebrities.[67] It makes sense that those who have an understanding of food, and a deep level of understanding of your product, or a particular aspect of its production, make the most credible and genuine spokespeople.

The hardware chain Bunnings has been using it's own staff as spokespeople in its advertising for many years. As workers within the business, these people provide a level of credibility that's difficult to match by using external voices. They are also the faces of 'real' people, another effective way to build trust and a closer relationship with consumers. Without careful selection, using an external voice to represent your brand can simply create another barrier to authenticity and transparency, rather than enhancing it.

Figure 8 depicts the key considerations when selecting the best spokespeople to communicate your food values.

Figure 8: Selecting your spokespeople

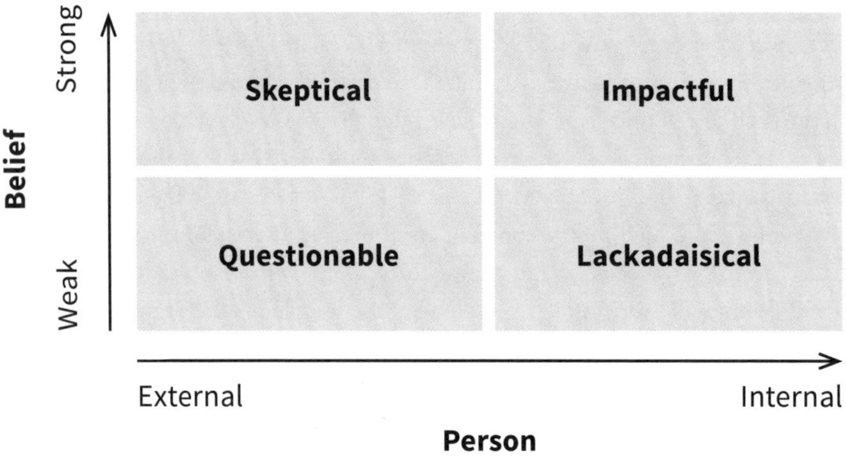

Consider your spokespeople and where they sit right now. The key considerations in each quadrant are as follows:

1. Questionable. Using an external person who has only a limited belief in your food related values is the weakest strategy, given the public mood today. If you use someone to speak on your behalf, they must believe in what you believe in. Otherwise you put your brand at risk, rather than amplifying your voice in a meaningful way.

2. Skeptical. If you decide to use an external person who strongly shares your food values, consumer skepticism will still play a role. People know an external spokesperson is paid for their endorsement and their authenticity may therefore still be questioned. So, while they may be a good fit, it may be difficult to create the degree of connection with consumers that your brand needs if it is aiming to inspire attention, rather than your having to constantly create attention.

3. Lackadaisical. Selecting an internal person to communicate your food values provides a more genuine, authentic voice in the market. However, it is critical that you find those within your business who are true believers, who share the values you have created and are passionate about what you stand for. Without this element, the communications you make could lack impact.

4. Impactful. To be impactful by inspiring consumers to pay attention to what you stand for, select spokespeople who are passionate about your food values and commitments, and have expertise in the areas of relevance. This provides the ideal combination. Those who truly believe in your food values and can communicate in a way that is naturally genuine and authentic will be those who will resonate with consumers and provide the power and energy that inspires their attention.

A Passionate Voice Shakes Up the Yoghurt Category

The story of Chobani offers a good example of the effective combination of values and a credible voice. Chobani yoghurt was launched in 2007 in the United States out of an old Kraft yoghurt plant that had closed in 2005. Within 10 years the company had reached US$2 billion in sales.[68] Chobani's founder had initially identified that the quality of yoghurt sold in the US was inferior to that in his home country of Turkey. The company declared its purpose as about 'bringing better quality food to more people'. There was no mainstream advertising, but the quality of the product along with the company's stated purpose were sufficient to inspire people to buy it – and keep buying it.

The spokesperson behind the brand is its creator, Hamdi Ulukaya, who is passionate about the product and has a deep understanding of all aspects of its production. He clearly articulates the company's purpose, the production process, the art of yoghurt making and its history. He embodies and communicates the values of the brand, and its authenticity and integrity. The combination of clear values and a credible and passionate voice are a winning combination.

More than One

Depending on the size and complexity of your business, you may need more than one spokesperson. Ideally, spokespeople who can talk about their area of the business with the depth of understanding required to meet consumer expectations will make the greatest contribution. Wherever the passionate believers are, seek them out and support them to bring their voices to market. This will lead you toward the creation of a brand with greater meaning and an authentic and credible voice in the market.

The final chapters demonstrate the return generated from investing in your food philosophy, values and commitments. The remainder of the book highlights how all these elements can work together for you both internally and externally throughout your business.

PART 4:
FOR A BETTER FUTURE

'Marty, the future isn't written. It can be changed'.

Doc Emmett Brown

'A great business enhances the overall health and wellbeing of society'.

John Mackey

CHAPTER 8

THE ROI – RETURN ON INTEGRITY

Maintaining a vision for the future of food, developing your food centred values and cultivating an authentic voice in the market takes time and investment. However once these are in place you are well positioned to reap the rewards. Your vision, values and voice place you in a strong position to leverage the work you've done and to create a better future for your business, team, local community, stakeholders and customers while making a difference to the future health of the population and planet. You'll be standing on a strong platform on which to build meaning into your brands and business, in turn enhancing long term business performance.

Communicating authentically through your food centred values will advance your business in each of the areas shown in figure 9.

Figure 9: The benefits of food values.

1. Build trust

'Trust is earned when actions meet words.'

Chris Butler

Once your food values are developed, you will be better placed to close any gaps that exist between how consumers believe you work and how you really do work. As mentioned earlier, research by the Centre for Food Integrity in the US has found that to generate trust, communicating through values is three to five times more effective than communicating through facts alone.[69] Communicating through values is therefore more effective than simply being transparent. Transparency is often approached primarily as a fact-driven communication activity however on its own, it is less effective at driving trust than communicating with values. Simon Sinek, in *Start with Why*[39], explains that 'trust is a feeling, not a rational experience'. So, providing more facts is only part of the solution.

Communicate through your food values and you will gradually gain trust. Applying your values to your communication strategy will enable you to engage effectively with consumers and customers and to create brand loyalty.

2. Make better and faster decisions

'It's not hard to make decisions once you know what your values are.'

Roy E. Disney

In a fast changing world with information overload, the ability to make fast and effective decisions is a critical skill. Having food centred values and commitments in place facilitates this ability. In his book *Amplifiers – the power of motivational leadership to inspire and influence*, Matt Church highlights how important it is that leaders are equipped to act quickly in this era of mass disruption.[70] While strategy is critical, he explains, now more than ever leaders need to be able to adapt and pivot easily. Adapting in the moment means being able to make fast and effective decisions.

Food values enable this to happen. Without the reference point they provide, the default can be to get locked into business-as-usual, basing decisions on how best to generate a short-term return using a short-term fix, relying on consumer-driven market research that in turn is subject to many variables, the whims of social media and the influence of the loudest voices. This risks losing brand positioning and value.

While profit and market research are both important, over-reliance on these two factors to guide decision making risks remaining in a me-too position in the market. It can also gradually result in a lack of long term consumer engagement and a reduced ability to undertake real innovation.

Decision making in the absence of food values and commitments can also lead to brand confusion across your portfolio, as happened for one client I worked with. The company had a varied range of children's products, and after auditing the nutritional profile to assess how well this matched the positioning of the products in the market it was clear there was significant confusion. The products ranged from an indulgent, fun treat, to an all-natural, locally produced product, to one that based its promotion on scientifically tested health benefits. The audit found the nutritional profile of the fun treat was 'healthier' than that of the 'naturally good' product. It was therefore not surprising that the marketing team were confused, as were the customers comparing their brands. Lack of clarity in decision making meant the range required reformulation and brand repositioning.

Clear food values enable teams to make quicker and better decisions. Consistency is driven by the beliefs held about the role your food plays in the lives of your customers and stakeholders, the community and the environment and this enables you to build a position in the market that is clear and valued.

3. Demonstrate consciousness

'In matters of style, swim with the current.
In matters of principle, stand like a rock.'

Thomas Jefferson

As global consciousness continues to evolve around how we live our lives, food businesses that have in place demonstrable values will have a competitive advantage over those that don't. The opportunity to generate shared value with consumers by demonstrating a higher level of consciousness in business is recognised by some of the world's largest food companies. In recent years, as outlined in earlier chapters, many have shifted their focus to embrace a vision that includes playing a role in solving some of the big-picture problems related to food. Being part of the solution to food-related problems has been a pivotal point of difference for many food businesses in recent years. Many new food businesses have launched with food related values in place that include local sourcing of ingredients, sustainability and being influencers of the food supply.

In her book *Conscious Marketing*, Carolyn Tate talks about the emergence of cause leadership as a business strategy. Cause leadership is about taking a stand on an issue that matters, role modelling the change and inviting people to participate in the journey.[71] It's about moving from the notion of profit to the idea of prosperity.

The CEO of Danone, Emmanuel Faber, is role modelling this approach within this major multinational company. In a speech to a Consumer Goods Forum in Berlin in June 2017[72], he noted how the food industry had let market forces drive demand and supply. '*Now,*' he suggested, '*the industry needs to work harder on health and sustainability, take stock of where the food system is, and be transparent with explaining to consumers why the industrialised food system is the way it is.*'

Danone have made a number of public commitments to improving the environment, including setting a target of net zero carbon and establishing the Livelihoods Fund, which invests in projects that sequester carbon within forests and restored natural ecosystems. Their Livelihoods Fund for Family Farming helps implement projects that restore degraded environments while also supporting the livelihoods of small farmers.

Significantly, Faber acknowledged that many companies are starting to act now because not doing so risks the bottom line. '*With more consumers voting with their wallets when it comes to health and sustainability, this is helping to focus the minds of many business leaders and the investment community.*'

This approach to business is an example of an evolving corporate consciousness about the way things were in the past, and the role food businesses can play to fix the problems and build a healthier and more sustainable food supply for the future.

Your food values demonstrate your consciousness around issues of importance to consumers therefore supporting you to create greater brand meaning.

4. Create greater team engagement

'A team aligned behind a vision will move mountains.'

Kevin Rose

Engaged employees are good for business. In *Drive*, Daniel Pink[10] notes the dearth of engagement in the modern workplace and quotes a Gallup research poll that found more than 50 per cent of employees in the US are not engaged at work, with nearly 20 per cent being actively disengaged.[73] The cost of disengagement was estimated at about US$300 billion a year in lost productivity. This is not the worst of it, though. According to a McKinsey and Co report, only 2 to 3 per cent of the workforce are highly engaged in their work.

Raj Sisodia, co-author of the book Conscious Capitalism[73], warned in 2012 that with trust in business having reached record lows, people are more cynical and wary, in turn affecting employee engagement. If engagement means caring about what you do even a little bit, this data indicates most workers don't care about their work, which makes it harder for them to be creative or innovative, to serve customers and to do truly extraordinary things.

The ability of companies to engage their employees is therefore a key to higher productivity and greater work satisfaction, with consequent lower staff turnover.

Research has found that the most highly motivated people, and those who are most productive and satisfied, are those who feel they are working for a cause they believe in that is larger than themselves.[80] A sense of purpose attached to your work provides the energy that drives intrinsic motivation. The high levels of worker disengagement that many companies struggle with can be addressed significantly by engaging individuals through a higher purpose. Food related values provide a means of expressing an authentic purpose.

Lack of engagement at work can also drive a lack of trust — a problem not restricted to consumers and customers but one that can also be occurring inside company walls.

When researching his book *Fat, Salt, Sugar*, Michael Moss[37] found many of the food industry executives he spoke with didn't eat the food produced by their own businesses. In my own work with one of my clients, I also found that many employees in the company held views about their food that aligned with myths spread on the internet that lacked any scientific evidence.

Engaging your team by standing behind your food values has the potential to enhance both engagement and productivity.

For businesses striving for greater meaning, best practice or a leadership position in the market, generating greater customer, stakeholder and team engagement is essential. This may mean offering something more than a great product or service or a competitive wage to generate greater engagement and loyalty. With 84% of millennials stating 'meaning' is more important than recognition, the opportunity is significant for food businesses to facilitate greater team engagement by creating a meaningful workplace based on the adoption of food centred values.[74]

5. The confidence to lead

'I was once afraid of people saying, "who does she think she is?" Now I have the courage to stand and say, "this is who I am".

Oprah Winfrey

To reduce risk, it can be tempting to follow rather than lead. When it comes to new product development, innovation, marketing, product-related claims and campaigns we often see food brands following each other's concepts, leading to a crowded 'me too' market.

That's not to say there aren't benefits in following. The advantages of following include lowering risk, greater confidence before acting and, potentially, greater efficiencies if you copy what someone else has already done. The problem with following, however, is that it risks skipping the understanding stage, and understanding is how you grow and lead.

Growth and leadership is facilitated through your food philosophy. It enables you to differentiate and to make decisions without worrying about what others are doing. All your decision making will be based on your values, rather than 'keeping up with the Joneses'. This can save time by enabling you to get on with what you are doing, rather than reacting to external noise. Your food values give you the confidence to lead and to go in your own direction.

6. Leapfrog competitors

'You can't look at the competition and say you are going to do it better. You have to look at the competition and say you are going to do it differently.'

Steve Jobs

Like most businesses operating in a competitive market, you no doubt keep a close eye on competitors. Often a lot of energy and time goes into this exercise. It's likely you assess each of the new products your competitors bring into the market, the claims they make and their marketing campaigns. You might even critique them and inform regulatory bodies of any possible non-compliance. Monitoring your competitors can distract you from your business, though. Being clear about your own food-related values will keep you focused on your own path, independent of what your competitors are doing. If Chobani had focused on the competitive and crowded yoghurt market in the US, it might not have launched at all. Rather, it focused on bringing better food to more people, and as a result was able to leapfrog competitors and grow to take the second highest share of the total yoghurt market by 2017.[68]

Focusing on your values will help you create efficiencies, get to market faster, generate greater consumer loyalty and engagement, and ultimately leapfrog your competitors.

7. Differentiate your brand

'In differentiation, not uniformity, lies the path of progress.'

Louis D. Brandeis

Food providers without a food philosophy must compete based on other features or benefits, such as price, convenience, the presence or absence of specific ingredients, health-related attributes and taste. While they are all important, relying on these features and benefits alone can make it harder to differentiate. Depending on your product range and offering, your competitors may be able to develop products or incorporate particular messages in the same way you do. This makes it harder to maintain a competitive advantage and a point of difference in the market over the long term.

Food values enable you to communicate what you are committed to and how you are different. They elevate you from being a 'me too' product by providing a broad, overarching point of difference. Your products could be similar to your competitors', but your food values will make you unique.

Look at businesses that take a stand for something, and it's easy to see that they 'stand out'. Nudie Juice stands for being 'creators of good' with commitments around their products never containing any 'nasties'. Ben and Jerry's have product-related values that signify their commitment to incorporating wholesome, natural ingredients in their products while also promoting business practices that respect the Earth. They also take a stand for marriage equality, climate justice and fair trade. While many ice creams are made with natural ingredients, not so many are also committed to the causes that Ben and Jerry stand for, which makes them unique in the ice-cream market. It's the communication of their values that differentiates their brand from their competitors.

The investment you make in establishing your food values will provide a strong return on integrity over time. This in turn provides a solid platform for future business growth and long term customer loyalty.

CHAPTER 9

THE PROOF: VISION, VALUES AND VOICE IN PRACTICE

Many of the world's leading food businesses have made changes or are in the process of making changes to adopt food centred values that reflect who they are and what they believe in. Small and medium-sized businesses are doing the same, with many launching into the market with clear values already in place, or that are naturally a reflection of who they are and what they stand for. Following are some examples of food values in action. This short list illustrates how some of the ideas discussed in this book are being actioned by those in the business of food.

Harris Farm Markets

Harris Farm Markets is a local Australian, family-owned and run food retailing business that commenced in 1971 with one store in an outer Sydney suburb. At the time of writing, the business has grown to 26 stores across Sydney and NSW. Employing 1500 people and serving 250,000 people a week, it has remained family owned and operated in a competitive and price-driven market.

Harris Farm state they have always believed in something greater than selling fresh food. Sitting at the core of their corporate values is the idea of fairness and this translates through to their customer focused message of: *'We're for the greater goodness'*.

The company's values cross each of the four areas of the food values model. They include the belief that fresh food brings families together and supports both communities and farmers, and that it offers nutrients to our bodies and joy to our taste buds. They consistently seek ways to reduce plastic packaging, and to deliver fairness to both the farmer and producer and to their customers.

One of Harris Farm's core values is to reconnect Australians with the joy of food, and this means they use Mother Nature as a guide to make decisions, such as what produce will be on special the next day. Rather than planning ahead and manufacturing a special a week out, they will use the logic of 'if it's in season, seize it'. In this way, according to Co-CEO Tristan Harris, the company can, *"deliver genuinely low prices on certain seasonal items because the product is abundant. When it is highly available, a lower price will not ruin everybody in the supply chain on the way through, you're just getting what Mother Nature throws at you. Rolling with the view that we can react quickly to the market helps us to remain honest with what we provide to the customer".*

The company's food centred values have enabled them to express their corporate values in a way that resonates and connects with their customers. Their values are a true reflection of the people behind the business and these values guide decision making and drive innovative thinking that is centred on solving problems to enable them to deliver to their values. Operating their business according to their values contributes to team engagement and the creation of 'good' based on win-win scenarios between their business, suppliers and growers, and their customers.

Earlier we noted one significant way that Harris Farm translated their food values into action. While mainstream supermarkets in Australia were selling milk for $1 per litre, Harris Farm made a commitment not to do this, recognising that the practice did not return a fair price to dairy farmers. The company introduced a 'love local' section in their stores, stocking produce sourced from within 150 km of the store. They also sell 'imperfect picks' — fruit and vegetables discounted by up to 50 per cent, and 'curious cuts' - cuts of meat that make use of the whole animal - encouraging a reduction in the amount of food lost through the supply chain.

In an interview with Tristan Harris, he highlighted many ways in which the company's values are reflected in their operations. The following provides an excerpt from this interview.

Lessons from Tristan Harris – 'Nature's going to give you the cue':

"I think you have to do this (develop and work by your values) because it's a reflection of who you are, versus doing it to get more customers. If you can reflect your true purpose, the true core of your business then customers will engage with that because they can sniff out something that's not authentic.

It can be hard however to keep control of your values as you get more volume in your business – particularly in food. The smaller your business the more authentic it almost is by its very nature. You get someone who's making muffins in their kitchen and they're not going to go and get 40 different types of gums and antioxidants, they're just going to make muffins. It's going to be authentic. So as you start to get bigger, that's the critical inflection point – that's the time to start and to make sure you are expanding for all the right reasons. This is when you need to have some core values and beliefs you can hang onto for the rest of your business life to say, 'this is what this product is about'. It's about having a bloody good product and it will always seem appropriate to make the product cheaper because you know that the volume is there but if you have to degrade the values of the business in order to do that, that is the slow cancer that sets into your business".

The value of values:

Because it's a little bit harder, doesn't mean you have to vanilla it. Try and stay authentic, try and stay genuine and use a bit of ingenuity to get to where you want to be. That I think has lead to the whole 'let's be different' to the other guys in the market. You know what, trying to work out a way to get out of the plastic is difficult but if we work hard at it, then we will be different from what the others will be and we will be living to our values and some customers, not all, will really gravitate toward that.

The benefits of the 'greater goodness'

'For the greater goodness' is what we saw as our marriage between the quality aspects of our business and how we like to operate. And where ingenuity really comes into it because if you deliver a better quality product that's one thing but if you can do it with a social purpose or with that extra hook you get some really beautiful outcomes. This is where you just look at something slightly differently and suddenly everybody wins a little bit more and they're the ones that are difficult to find but the Imperfect Picks is one of them. You just go, well hang on a second, there's all of this fruit that we're not selling, we were putting it in buckets, but it was losing its vibe, and the fruit was just getting cheaper and cheaper and more and more of it was going to waste, so coming out and saying this fruit does look terrible but eat it – it eats exactly the same, there's nothing wrong with it and people were like 'oh, so it's cheaper, but it is the same so I save money and its more sustainable and the farmer earns if I buy it' – solved.

There's a few of those sorts of things. Like when we first did our campaign on plastic bags we were thinking 'should we charge for plastic bags' and we were like, we know the customers will leave us if we do that. Then one of my brothers came up with the idea 'how about we pay the customer to not take the plastic bag'? But then we realised that it's only less than a cent for a bag and if a customer uses 3 bags it's only going to be 2 cents and that's not really compelling for them. So what we did is we said that if anybody doesn't use a plastic bag, we'll donate 5 cents to Clean Up Australia and that just changed people's attitude toward using plastic bags. So that's a big way we've changed the problem – just giving a little bit of a reminder, a little bit of incentive to customers to walk away from plastic bags and just use fruit boxes – we have hundreds of these and they're going to recycling everyday anyway so if the customer uses them and they go home and they get recycled then it's not going to live in the waste stream forever.

So that's another good way and that's where a lot of the thinking about the 'greater goodness' really came from because if we work hard enough and if we have smart enough people around us who can think through those sort of problems we will come up with those sorts of solutions which are much better for everyone.

Being authentic

I guess we just keep on doing it because it's a true reflection of who we are and what we want to be, as opposed to something we do for getting that customer bump. Businesses having a social purpose has become very de-rigour lately and I reckon if you go out and say 'right we've got to have a purpose' and a company that makes sheet metal fabrication says our purpose is blah and they just manufacture something on the spot I don't think that gives you anything – I don't think it improves the life of your employee, I don't think it makes your customer more engaged, I don't think there's really anything valuable in that. So I think if it is your true purpose, your true core of your business then customers will engage with that because they can sniff out something that's not authentic.

A view on food culture

Food should be a positive part of your life. The least manufactured and the less mass marketed, highly marketed it is, the closer you get to a time and culture where food was important and food was connecting and food was all of the things that instinctively everyone in the world knows about. You know there aren't many things that everyone in the world does, but eating is one of them".

Brasserie Bread

Brasserie Bread is a foodservice wholesale supplier launched in 2000 that provides artisan sourdough loaves, Italian bread, rolls, pastries and cakes to cafes, restaurants, hotels, caterers and airlines. The company was founded by Head Baker Michael Klausen and Tony Pappas from Allpress Coffee with the aim of mastering the art of an authentic sourdough bread. Since commencing operations, the company has expanded to open new premises in Sydney's south, as well as bakeries in Melbourne and Queensland. Brasserie Bread launched Australia's first single origin sourdough bread and have been pioneering a 'grain first' approach to bread that elevates the importance of the nutritional value of the grain, while also creating a stronger connection between the farmer and consumers.

According to Michael Klausen, *"Any food business with a certain amount of volume has a responsibility to contribute toward a better future. There is a point at which you need to decide – are you going to contribute to making a better future or are you going to squeeze the lemon? Many people don't know how to go into this world but working from within a business means you can inspire this".*

Michael has been inspiring change over the past 20 years and as a result, is making a difference to the lives of farmers, to the environment through the types of seeds he has encouraged them to grow, to the nutritional value of the bread the company bakes and to the social connection that food facilitates through conducting baking education classes for kids and adults.

Below is Michael's viewpoint on how food centred values drive Brasserie Breads operation and philosophy:

"In our business most of our investment, other than what we spend on our people, goes into our grain. For me, I've always wanted to know where food came from so when I started to look into bread, I was surprised to find that no-one was mentioning the source of the grain. I went to millers and asked for access to the farmers but they didn't want to provide this. I planted the idea with them that the grain was critical to the flavour of the bread and that maybe we should grow for flavour rather than yield but the millers didn't want to have a bar of it so I went straight to the farmers myself. They thought I was mad. But when I spoke to them in a different way – that they could create a better future for their children by caring for the soil better - they became a little bit interested. What I learnt was that if a farmer takes an environmental approach they often don't get paid for it. So when I said I could appreciate their hard work and that they could get paid for it then they thought it was an interesting idea. Once they knew they had a market, the farmers then became more involved in the project than we did. It became a two way street.

Farming for a better future

We have been able to use our buying power to start working with the farmer to change the type of wheat to be better placed for the future. Ninety five percent of our wheat goes overseas but none has been developed for nutrition and flavor. It's all been developed for yield.

What I am interested in is how a farm with good soil can use modern technology to work out how to deliver wheat varieties that have flavor and nutrition. These two things are often combined -they are related to each other as the stuff that impacts flavor often contributes a high level of nutrition.

Seeds for a better future

I've found two seed breeders who have been able to change the varieties of wheat so that it's drought proof, pest resistant and the right height. To find these we have had to go back in time and look at heirloom varieties to get all the things we need.

The idea is then to find in the DNA of the heirloom wheat what indicates the high level of nutrition and flavor and go from there. Having the bakery behind it helps as this provides a market. This means we can provide an incentive for the farmers. One of the keys for us is that the farmer needs to understand soil health and this is happening now. A modern farmer has different education and believes it's a waste of money to have to use artificial spray and doesn't want to work in this environment. They are now actively avoiding this.

Values vs value

Decisions often come down to money but then we need to ask what are the benefits? Our relationship with the farmers is a win-win. Farmers can tell a story about Brasserie Bread -they can talk to their neighbours, schools and community.

Farmers have found that their association with us has made their business unique – they are aware of the brand and the connection is strong. Traceability and understanding different farms give different flavours makes single source wheat an exciting and growing area.

People ask how we find a market. I think things are changing. Australian consumers want traceability. You see this in meat where the meat industry has found a need for brands – consumers want this. You can charge more for the meat if its value added so it's good for the farmer and for business.

It's not always easy but we are changing the future. By working hard to buy this product from the farmer we are pushing him to make a better product. Neighbours look over the fence and can see that it actually works. It's a 4-5 year process to change the land but it is happening.

We're now looking at an ancient style of grain called emma – it's not cheap but we have no problem selling it.

Vision for the future

I would like to see a future where farmers get paid for their grain based on its nutritional value – the higher the nutritional value, the more you get paid for it. If we think of it from a survival point of view it makes sense – the point of eating is to give us nutrition. This is very current thinking. Younger chefs have a social awareness and are doing more good. For example, food waste is being attacked in both small scale and large scale ways. There is more education happening through restaurants and classes because we have come so far apart from the origins of our food.

In 2018, we became the first contestant from the professional bakery division and the first finalist to win both the Royal Agricultural Society's President's Medal and the NSW Department of Primary Industries Innovation award. It feels good to be recognized in this way, along with all the people who have been willing to come with us on this journey.

Today we can now put a loaf of bread on the table and tell you what paddock it is from and that is extremely important.

Danone

Danone is one of the world's largest food companies, generating over €20 billion in sales annually, primarily from fresh dairy, infant and toddler, water and medical nutrition products. The company was formed as the result of a merger between BSN and Gervais Danone in 1972. It was in that same year that the company's CEO recognised the importance of corporate social responsibility, laying the groundwork for the various projects funded by the company in this area since.

While Danone has long held an interest in funding nutrition research and established the Danone Institute to further knowledge in this area, in recent years it has broadened its focus to adopt wider initiatives and values. These include recognising and acting in areas where its practices can influence not only personal and population health, but the health of the planet.

Danone's corporate values include the guiding internal principles of humanism, openness, proximity and enthusiasm. The company's food values include a belief that food can change the world, and that each time we eat and drink we are voting for the kind of world we want to live in. The company is committed to leading the 'Alimentation Revolution' around the way food is produced, marketed, designed and consumed, with the aim of protecting and nourishing the health of both people and planet. Danone has committed to be an agent of change through its belief that the food and water ecosystem needs to work in harmony with people, communities and the environment. The company also believes in creating a relationship with its 900 million customers that is a force for good.

Within this commitment Danone recognises the importance of the relationship between a healthy body and healthy food, and of resilient social structures. Under the umbrella signature of 'One Planet. One Health', Danone is aiming to use the power of food to change lives and the world. Examples of how this is playing out in the market include:

- committing to achieving zero net carbon status for Evian water by 2020
- educating and encouraging smallholders in Indonesia to switch to organic farming as a means of protecting the infiltration area and preserving water sources
- educating children on where milk comes from, how yoghurt is made, and the importance of caring for cows and the environment through farm visits and classroom lessons
- supporting small dairy farmers in Tunisia through training and access to modern equipment via micro-loans. This project strengthens the company's local supply chain while supporting the resilience of local communities.
- producing yoghurt in Bangladesh from locally sourced milk. The milk is then fortified to address micro-nutrient deficiencies in the area. The project also serves to create local employment opportunities.

Danone North America recently become the world's largest Certified B-Corporation®, a certification that recognises companies which are balancing shareholders financial interests with social and environmental considerations.

Sweet Earth Natural Foods

Sweet Earth Natural Foods was launched in 2012 by two former food and beverage industry executives. With starting funds of US$5 million, by 2016 the company had 200 employees and a turnover of US$25 million,[75] and distributed to more than 10,000 stores throughout the US. The product range is all vegetarian, although until recently was not specifically promoted as such, and includes burritos, artisan bowls, veggie burgers and breakfast sandwiches.

The company started with a clear set of values related to their food and the way it is produced. These values include:

- ***'Honour and sustain the land.*** *Crafting food is how we stay mindful of the Earth. We choose ingredients that sustain and protect our coast. And we prepare dishes honouring the fact that all around the world, unique cultures celebrate their lands with food, revering its health and nutrition.*
- ***Cultivate a curious mind and palate.*** *We are food explorers. The Sweet Earth Kitchen is a magic temple where passionate chefs bring together ancient recipes and today's harvest. The result? Food that you'll love, that'll surprise you, that'll satisfy what we all believe: food should be delicious. It should add zest to your day and spice to your mind. We put in your hands an incredible diversity of plant foods and cooking traditions.*
- ***Sustain a healthy body.*** *We believe food traditions endure for a reason — they allow us to thrive. Millennia have taught cultures what works, and at Sweet Earth we are doing our best to listen. And here's what we've learned: interesting flavours, vibrant colours, and complex textures are best for our bodies. Follow your nose to those and there you will find protein, vitamins, probiotics, fatty acids, fibres, it goes on! Inventive cooking means nutritious living. The best for your body: that's our passion.'*

In 2017, the success of the business saw it sold to Nestle for an undisclosed sum.

Whole Foods Market

Whole Foods Market is a supermarket-style grocery chain that was launched in the US in 1980. The company started as a merger of two natural food stores employing a total of 19 people. The business grew through mergers and acquisitions, along with new stores. The company now has 468 stores and is a world leader in natural and organic foods. It was purchased by Amazon in July 2017 for US$14 billion. Whole

Foods Market is a food business with a strong sense of purpose and longstanding food values that include:

- *We sell the highest quality natural organic products available.*
- *We satisfy, nourish and delight our customers.*
- *We promote the health of our stakeholders through healthy eating education.*

These values translate into:

- *a list of ingredients that are unacceptable in our food*
- *commitments to animal welfare and sustainable seafood*
- *providing loans to small, local producers.*

The company has established numerous initiatives across its supply chain. It has also created the Whole Kids Foundation, Whole Planet Foundation, and the Whole Cities Foundation. These Foundations fund projects to empower some of the world's poorest people with micro-credit to help lift them out of poverty, they administer a school gardens grant program and also aim to improve individual and community health through increasing access to nutritious food in the communities within which they operate.

Barilla

Barilla is an Italian based food company making products including pasta, pasta sauces, meal solutions and bakery products with distribution in over 100 countries worldwide. It was founded in Parma in 1877 by Pietro Barilla and remains an Italian family owned company today. Barilla is the world's leading pasta brand, employs more than 8,000 people and claims that 120 Barilla products are sold worldwide every second.

Barilla's food related values are outlined in the three major areas of:

Good for you

Improving peoples wellbeing with a commitment that by 2020 this will occur as a result of promoting food choices that are in line with the food pyramid.

Good for the planet

Reducing the company's impact on the planet with a commitment that by 2020 it will only provide people with food that sits at the base of the environmental pyramid.

Good for communities

Enabling inclusion of all with a commitment that by 2020 it will promote food access programs, educational paths and leverage diversities.

Barilla supports the above values with specific commitments linked to its food including:

- Commitments to nutrition such as assisting people to adopt eating patterns consistent with the principles of the Mediterranean diet; supporting nutrition research and the application of new findings in the area of health and nutrition to its operations and in a way that anticipates people's needs; providing products consistent with specific nutritional guidelines
- Commitments to the environment such as the provision of products that help reduce emissions and consumption of resources in the company's factories; and reaching a goal of sourcing 100% of their strategic raw materials responsibly and from sustainable supply chains.

The company reports on the progress it is making toward these objectives, including the amount of saturated fat, sugar and sodium it has removed from the foods it makes and the amount of water, energy and CO2 emissions it has saved as a result of adopting new operating practices.

Barilla's reported operating profit for 2016 was 380 million euro, an increase on the previous year arising as a result of continual growth in sales volume and revenue[76].

Sweetgreen

Sweetgreen is a casual fast food chain in the US launched in 2007 by three university graduates. It has around 80 stores and offers a range of salads and bowls featuring fresh, local and seasonal ingredients. Its mission is to inspire healthier communities by connecting people to real food. The company's food ethos incorporates commitments to scratch cooking, transparency through working with farmers who are doing the right thing and highlighting who they are within their stores, sustainability from store design to waste management, local sourcing and food safety. The company has received funds from investment firm Revolution Growth and has raised US$95 million to date.

Laneway Greens

Started by two brothers, Laneway Greens is a small business that opened its first salad bar style store in Melbourne in 2015. The store serves salads, pressed juices and smoothies and their mission is to reconnect their customers with the food they are eating. The menu is seasonal with the dishes cooked from scratch using simple food, sourced from transparent supply chains, that is produced sustainably and with minimal impact on the environment.

The business runs according to the following food philosophy:

'We believe the freshest produce comes from the best farming. We believe in seasonal supply not consumer demand. We believe in building a community through our kitchens. We believe less hands make honest food. We believe our local farmers = our local community. We believe food is a chance to connect. We believe in influencing the way food is produced.'

Two years after launch, a second store opened, with a third soon to be added to meet demand for food produced according to this philosophy.

'The tools that we use to change the world ought to be beautiful in themselves. It's not just enough to survive. We've got to make something better than what we've got. And I think that we will'.

Alex Steffen

A FINAL WORD

I began this book by highlighting how rising global consciousness is affecting how business is being conducted and is leading to an evolution in consumer values around purchasing decisions. This evolution is providing significant opportunities for food businesses. Now is the right time to take a fresh look at how food is produced and marketed and how this is communicated to consumers. With obesity and other lifestyle-related diseases on the rise, environmental collapse threatening the quality of life of future generations, and the social and cultural threads of society being placed under pressure, the development of food centred values can play a powerful role in creating a better future for people and the planet, while elevating brands from a 'me too' market position to one that is more meaningful.

Those in the business of food have both a responsibility and an opportunity to use their purchasing power, influence and voice to lead for change. This is not only about the health of the community; it's also about long-term business success. With rising consciousness, people are increasingly shifting their purchasing preferences toward businesses that are seen to be behaving ethically and acting with integrity. Preparing for the future means preparing for a 'better future'. This requires food businesses to adopt both conscious corporate values and responsible and consistent values around the food they produce.

People care about the food they eat, but eating is about more than nourishment. Working according to strong and ethical food values provides companies with an opportunity to demonstrate their understanding of this while also providing a key way to differentiate in a crowded market. Food values address the deficit in trust in the food system, provide companies with the confidence to speak out and educate, create a greater connection between the company brand and the consumer, and enable businesses to make faster and more effective decisions. Food values enable companies to move on from the fight for shelf space based on price, to becoming more proactive in leading people to a better place, where quality is valued over quantity and connection is valued over convenience.

The smartest food businesses focus on solving food-related problems rather than simply selling food, and in doing so, help create a brighter, healthier future for all.

Food for a Better Future has been about inspiring a new direction for the global business of food - one that recognises food as a solution to some of the big challenges currently facing society, while also building a platform for future business success.

To stay in touch and be kept informed of my latest thinking, please visit my website and sign up for my Perspectives on the Future of Food www.sharonnatoli.com/blog

You will also find details on my latest programs and events and I would be happy to hear from you with any thoughts or comments you have as you have read through this book.

Endnotes

1. Horizon Media Finger on the Pulse Study, 2016

2. Havas Media Group. Meaningful Brands Index, 2017

3. Kotter, 'Can you handle an exponential rate of change?', *Forbes*, 19 July 2011, https://www.forbes.com/sites/johnkotter/2011/07/19/can-you-handle-an-exponential-rate-of-change/#1c6d64f04eb0.

4. Dave Donnan, Randy Burt , Laurie Demeritt and David Hokens, 'Is big food in trouble?', *ATKearney & The Hartman Group*, 2016, http://store.hartman-group.com/content/is-big-food-in-trouble-2016.pdf.

5. Andrew Borrell, 'As global food demand rises, climate change is hitting our staple crops', *The Conversation*, 1 March 2017, https://theconversation.com/as-global-food-demand-rises-climate-change-is-hitting-our-staple-crops-73360.

6. Brittany Patterson, Australia's Farmers Challenged by Climate Change, Scientific American, 19 March 2015. https://www.scientificamerican.com/article/australia-s-farmers-challenged-by-climate-change/

7. United Nations. World population predicted to reach 9.8billion by 2050 and 11.2 billion in 2100, Sustainable Development Goals. 2017.

8. Stefan Hajkowicz *Global Mega-trends: Seven Patterns of Change Shaping Our Future*. CSIRO Publishing, 2015

9. Andrew Ross Sorkin, 'BlackRock's message: contribute to society, or risk losing our support', *The New York Times*, 15 January 2018,

10. Daniel Pink, 2011. *Drive: The Surprising Truth about What Motivates Us*. Canongate Books.

11. L Trahan, K Stuebing, M Hiscock, J Fletcher. The Flynn Effect: A meta-analysis. Psychol Bull 2014. 140(5): 1332-1360

12. Chris Pash, "Ethical investing' funds now top $600 billion in Australia, with returns starting to match the market', *Business Insider Research*, 25 July 2017. https://www.businessinsider.com.au/ethical-investing-funds-australia-2017-7.

13. Unilever, 'Report shows a third of consumers prefer sustainable brands', *Unilever*, 5 January 2017, https://www.unilever.com/news/Press-releases/2017/report-shows-a-third-of-consumers-prefer-sustainable-brands.html.

14. https://www.unilever.com/sustainable-living/values-and-values/ Accessed 11 May 2018

15. Report shows a third of consumers prefer sustainable brands. 5 January 2017. https://www.unilever.com/news/Press-releases/2017/report-shows-a-third-of-consumers-prefer-sustainable-brands.html

16. World Health Organisation, 'Obesity and overweight', *World Health Organisation*, reviewed February 2018, http://www.who.int/mediacentre/factsheets/fs311/en/.

17. Arnhem, 'Mindful choices: the key food driver for 2018, says Innova Market Insights', *PR Newswire*, 9 November 2017, https://www.prnewswire.com/news-releases/mindful-choices-the-key-food-driver-for-2018-says-innova-market-insights-656335853.html.

18. IPSOS FoodCHATs. Annual report 2015-2016.

19. Elizabeth Crawford, '6 steps companies can take to 'do good' and expand their appeal to modern consumers', *Food Navigator*, 29 November 2016, http://www.foodnavigator-usa.com/Suppliers2/6-steps-to-take-to-do-good-and-expand-appeal-to-modern-consumers.

20. Jenny Goldie and Katherine Betts (eds), 2014. *Sustainable Futures: Linking Population, Resources and the Environment*. CSIRO Publishing.

21. United Nations Sustainable Development Goals. Goal 12. Responsible consumption and production patterns.

22. Ben Cooper, 'The food industry in 2018 - bolder aims, broader horizons for sustainability', *Just-Food*, 1 January 2018, https://www.just-food.com/analysis/the-food-industry-in-2018-bolder-aims-broader-horizons-for-sustainability_id138244.aspx.

23. Paul Polman, 'Paul Polman on fixing a broken food system', *The Wall Street Journal*, 17 January 2018, https://www.wsj.com/amp/articles/paul-polman-on-fixing-a-broken-food-system-1516200607?__twitter_impression=true.

24. Marine Stewardship Council. Australian consumers prefer sustainable seafood. Oct 2016. https://www.msc.org/newsroom/news/australian-consumers-prefer-sustainable-seafood

25. Brooke Barton, 'Shareholders target food sector supple chain risks', *Ceres*, 26 June 2017, https://www.ceres.org/news-center/blog/shareholders-target-food-sector-supply-chain-risks.

26. Steven Bird, 'Computing gives us tools to preserve disappearing languages', *The Conversation*, 14 June 2016, https://theconversation.com/computing-gives-us-tools-to-preserve-disappearing-languages-60235.

27. Gabbacia DR. We are what we eat: ethnic food and the making of Americans. Cambridge, MA. Harvard University Press, 2009.

28. Burlingham B. Presentation on biodiversity, Dietitians Association of Australia webinar, June 2016.

29. Mason, P and Lang T. Sustainable Diets. How ecological nutrition can transform consumption and the food system. Routledge, Oxon, 2017.

30. Zachary Davies Boren, 'There are officially more mobile devices than people in the world', *Independent*, 7 October 2014, http://www.independent.co.uk/life-style/gadgets-and-tech/news/there-are-officially-more-mobile-devices-than-people-in-the-world-9780518.html.

31. Deloitte. Smart everything, everywhere. Mobile Consumer Survey 2017. The Australia Cut.

32. Julia Carrie Wong, 'Former Facebook executive: social media is ripping society apart', *The Guardian*, 13 December 2017, https://www.theguardian.com/technology/2017/dec/11/facebook-former-executive-ripping-society-apart.

33. Utter J, Denny S, Robinson E, Fleming T, Ameratunga S and Grant S., 2013, Family meals and the well-being of adolescents, *J Paediatr Child Health*, Vol 49(11):906-11.

34. Australia's Health 2016. Web report, Sept 2016

35. Health Star Rating Advisory Committee, 'Two-year progress review report on the implementation of the Health Star rating system, June 2014 – June 2016', *Health Star Rating*, April 2017,

36. Jack Ringquist, Tom Phillips, Barb Renner, Rod Sides, Kristen Stuart, Mark Baum and Jim Flannery, 'Capitalizing on the shifting consumer food value equation', Deloitte, 2016, https://www2.deloitte.com/content/dam/Deloitte/us/Documents/consumer-business/us-fmi-gma-report.pdf.

37. Michael Moss 2013. *Salt, Sugar, Fat: How the Food Giants Hooked Us*. Random House, p. 11.

38. Anna Sanford, 'Millennials are saving the planet, one kale salad at a time', *AlterNet*, 18 June 2017, http://www.alternet.org/culture/millennials-are-saving-planet-one-kale-salad-time#.WUcuO029-pQ.twitter.

39. Simon Sinek. *Start with Why.* Penguin Group, 2009.

40. Tim Wu. The Tyranny of Convenience. The New York Times, 16 February 2018. https://www.nytimes.com/2018/02/16/opinion/sunday/tyranny-convenience

41. Alison Potter, 'Unpacking the foodprint from meal boxes', *Choice*, 14 June 2017, https://www.choice.com.au/food-and-drink/eating-out/fast-food/articles/meal-box-delivery-sustainability.

42. Cathy Siegner, 'Where will meal kits find future growth?', *Food Dive*, 18 October 2017, https://www.fooddive.com/news/grocery--where-will-meal-kits-find-future-growth/507506/.

43. The Hartman Group, 'As Snackification in Food Culture Becomes More Routine, Traditional Mealtimes Get Redefined', *The Hartman Group*, 16 February 2016, https://www.hartman-group.com/hartbeat/638/as-snackification-in-food-culture-becomes-more-routine-traditional-mealtimes-get-redefined.

44. The Hartman Group. The future of snacking, 2016 http://store.hartman-group.com/the-future-of-snacking-2016/

45. Justin Nel, Mintel, 2017. AIFST The Future of Food, conference presentation, July.

46. Jack Cain. Almost half of the people in Australia's cities are yet to order their food through an app. http://www.ausfoodnews.com.au/2018/04/30/almost-half-of-the-people-in-australias-cities-are-yet-to-order-their-food-through-an-app.html 30 April 2018.

47. David Gillespie, 2012. *Big Fat Lies: How the Diet Industry Is Making You Sick, Fat and Poor*. Penguin.

48. Gary Taubes, 2016. *The Case Against Sugar*. Portobello Books.

49. David Perlmutter, 2016. *The Grain Brain Whole Life Plan*. Little, Brown.

50. David Satterthwaite, Gordon McGranahan and Cecilia Tacoli, 2010, Urbanization and its implications for food and farming, *Philos Trans R Soc Lond B Biol Sci.*, Vol 27; 365(1554): 2809–2820.

51. Australian Bureau of Statistics '4102.0 - Australian social trends, Dec 2012', *Australian Bureau of Statistics*, 9 April 2013, http://www.abs.gov.au/AUSSTATS/abs@.nsf/Lookup/4102.0Main+Features10Dec+2012#Looking

52. Michael Pollan. In Defence of Food. 2008. Penguin Books.

53. Jenny Rooney. Why the ability to teach could be a key differentiator for brands: new research from VCU Brand Centre. Forbes online. 23 February 2016.

54. Elizabeth Crawford. Six steps companies can take to 'do good' and expand their appeal to modern consumers. Food Navigator, 29 Nov 2016 https://www.foodnavigator-usa.com/Article/2016/11/29/6-steps-to-take-to-do-good-and-expand-appeal-to-modern-consumers

55. IRi, 2017. 'Consumer Health: Unlocking the Growth Opportunities', September.

56. Datamonitor, 2013. 'Health & Wellness Trends in Food & Drink'.

57. 2018 Trends Webinar. Supermarket Guru

58. Nielsen, 2015. *We Are What We Eat. Healthy Eating Trends Around the World*, January.

59. Nancy Gagliardi, 'Consumers Want Healthy Foods- And Will Pay More for Them', *Forbes*, 18 February 2015, http://bit.ly/2mB1AZh.

60. Candy and Snack TODAY, "Five-Year Forecast: Protein Craze Winds Down," April 15, 2015 http://www.candyusa.com/news/five-year-forecast-protein-craze-winds-down/

61. 'SDG industry matrix- Food, beverage and consumer goods', *United Nations Global Compact & KPMG International Cooperative*, February 2016, https://home.kpmg.com/content/dam/kpmg/xx/pdf/2017/05/sdg-food-bev.pdf.

62. David McKinna, 'Big Food Goes Off', *Bluenotes*, 5 September 2017, https://bluenotes.anz.com/posts/2017/09/big-food-goes-off.

63. 'The seven countries study- About the study', *The seven countries study*, https://www.sevencountriesstudy.com/about-the-study/.

64. TED 2017. Susan Pinker. The secret to living longer may be your social life

65. Jamie Duncan, 'Arnott's Shapes: Consumer backlash forces flavour promise', *Herald Sun*, 29 April 2016, http://www.heraldsun.com.au/news/victoria/arnotts-shapes-consumer-backlash-forces-flavour-backdown/news-story/3b9a5acdce3117e3d5acdb7f74c04f6a.

66. NAB Chairman Dr Ken Henry AC – Speech to the AIC Governance Summit https://news.nab.com.au/nab-chairman-dr-ken-henry-ac-speech-to-the-aicd-governance-summit/ 2 March 2018

67. John Tylee, 'Are ads featuring real people more than a fad?', *Campaign Live*, 1 November 2016, https://www.campaignlive.co.uk/article/ads-featuring-real-people-fad/1413578.

68. Mary Ellen Shoup, 'Chobani beats Yoplait in sales and market share as Dannon takes No. 1 spot in US yogurt market', *Dairy Reporter*, 13 March 2017, https://www.dairyreporter.com/Article/2017/03/13/Chobani-surpasses-Yoplait-in-sales-and-market-share.

69. New consumer trust research- A dangerous disconnect: new CFI research IDS food and AG trust gaps', *Food Integrity*, http://www.foodintegrity.org/research/consumer-trust-research/current-research/.

70. Matt Church. 2013. *Amplifiers. The power of motivational leadership to inspire and influence*. Wiley.

71. Carolyn Tate, 2015. *Conscious Marketing: How to create an awesome business with a new approach to marketing*. Wiley.

72. Dean Best, 'Danone CEO Emmanuel Faber on why industry "mindset" on health and sustainability needs to change - just-food interview, part one', *Just-Food*, July 2017, https://www.just-food.com/interview/danone-ceo-emmanuel-faber-on-why-industry-mindset-on-health-and-sustainability-needs-to-change-just-food-interview-part-one_id137124.aspx.

73. John Mackay & Raj Sisodia. *Conscious Capitalism. Liberating the Heroic Spirit of Business*. Harvard Business School Publishing, 2014.

74. Ahmad Raza. Why a purpose driven mission is the key to motivating millennials. Entrepreneur, Dec 2016 https://www.entrepreneur.com/article/284857

75. Dale Buss, 'Sweet Earth's Sweet Growth: 5 Questions With CEO Kelly Swette', *Brand Channel*, 31 March 2017, http://brandchannel.com/2017/03/31/sweet-earth-5-questions-033117/.

76. Barilla Annual Report 2016.